Bravin Publishing

presents

WORD PLAY

Our Words Are Our Canvas

This is a work of fiction. Names, characters, places and incidents either are the product of the author's imagination or are used fictitiously, and any resemblance to actual persons, living or dead, business establishments, events, or locales is entirely coincidental.
WORD PLAY

A Bravin Publishing Book /Published by arrangement with the authors

Copyright © 2011 by BRAVIN PUBLISHING
Cover design by G8 Visual Designs
Interior Designed by Bravin Publishing, LLC

This book, or parts thereof, may not be reproduced in any form without permission. The scanning, uploading, and distribution of this book via the Internet or via any other means without the permission of the publisher is illegal and punishable by law. Please purchase only authorized electronic editions, and do not participate in or encourage electronic piracy of copyrighted materials. Your support of the author's rights is appreciated.

ISBN: 978-0-9845018-7-8

Bravin Publishing
PO Box 340317 Rochdale Village, New York 11434.
www.bravinpublishing.com

Printed in the United States of America

Table of Contents

KARAST IS 1
    Suicidal Hope 3
    A Mothers Tribute 4
    I Am America 5
    When I Was A Human Being 6
    Read Me A Passage 7
    Tell My Story 9
    Blind Faith In A Noose 11
    She Said I was Too Deep 12
    Kill 'Em Before They Grow 14
    She said His Abuse Felt like God Abandoned Her 15
    Paranoid 16

INFINITE 18
    Spoken Word 19
    She Gave Life 21
    Butterfly 22
    Dandelion 24
    Freedom Manifesto 27

J. Steven Williams aka "Tha Real" 31
    Better Than Me 33
    Collateral Damage 35
    IGNORANCE 37
    Mis-Praise of Man 38
    Right Here 39
    She Try (Housewife Blues) 40
    Thank You 41
    The Search 42
    They 43
    When I Push Out 44

Trevis Moore 46
    My Love Takes Flight 47
    A Poem To The Unborn (BLACK SEED) 49
    Mr. Right?(Can I Get A Cup Of Sugar?) 51

- Old Friends.. 53
- Brotha Man.. 55
- Yes, I Am back.. 57
- Ms. Love Me 59
- CUPID 61
- THE 63
- Don't It Hurt?... 64
- SHE 66

Empress Poetry..69
- Come Meet a Man... 70
- Who I Am 71
- NEO-Sistah... 73
- Farewell Endangered One 75
- Numbers 76
- From The Cave.. 77
- Lost 78
- You... 79
- The Sequel 81
- Your Kinda Love 83

Distinguish..86
- Trust... 87
- Analytical 89
- Boy Positive 90
- If I Was A Poet 92
- Her Stories Through History 94
- The Ankh... 95
- We Are The Liars Of The Truth 96
- The Black Woman's Standards 97
- Womentors.. 99
- Food For Thought 100

All Flowin' Big Mama..102
- Through these eyes 103
- Smarter Than a Fifth Grader....................................... 104

- For H.I.M. Verbal Waters 105
- Extend Your Hand Across the Sea 105
- Confidence 106
- Heartbeat of the City 107
- Defined 108
- Innocence's Prayer 109
- Broken Chains 111
- Untold 113

ARIES 115
- 1000 Kisses 116
- Apology 117
- I LISTEN 118
- Artistic Inspiration 119
- I Love You 120
- I'd Die 121
- Love Is An Emotion 122
- Marriage 123
- Nigger 124
- Rain 124
- Reality 125

K`larity 127
- The Queen 129
- Black Pearl 130
- Un-Chained Butterfly 131
- Even A Rose 132
- E.M.S. / Detox 133
- FREE 134
- Family Tree 134
- Washed Away 135
- I Wanna 137
- Lyrically Speaking 138
- Evolutionary Soldier 139

Anwar L. Counts 141
- (An) Urban Legend 142
- Black Like Me 143
- Eyedentity 144
- Hopping the Fence 145

I am who I am	147
Miracle of a Dream	148
My Brother's Keeper	149
Opportunity	150
Reflection of HiStory	151
Youth is Gold(en)	152
K. L. Belvin	154
THE DEATH OF THE RADICALS	155
Poetry Forgive Us	157
Racism	158
A DIVA	160
I Would Say I Do All Over Again	161
Transformation	163
Promises	164
Let it Go! (Ode to an Ex)	165
A Steward	166

KARAST IS
(Christ Is)

    Raised in Harlem New York and breast fed by the rough streets of sugar hill; Karast Is (an Egyptian/Kemetic concept for the western term Christ) was an aspiring cartoon artist who loved perusing the minds of great African artists and Poets. Like so many young Black males trapped in the squalid realms of ghetto reality, while at the same time striving to germinate into manhood without relevant fathers or father figures, Karast became prey to the vulture-like sadisms of the street life. As a result, it cost him over a decade of imprisonment in America's prison industrial complex.

    It was there where violence, fear, hate, racism and dehumanization is the acceptable norm, that Karast spiritually, politically, and poetically transformed himself into an educator; facilitating cultural awareness classes at Clinton, Elmira and Attica Correctional Facilities.

    In 1996, Karast began writing his first book, "From Universal Builder to Modern Day Destroyers" which addresses various issues concerning African people in American Society today. Active in his community, Karast is a part of "World Youth Movement for Global Peace" at Medgar Evers College in Brooklyn, where he is a psychology major. Karast utilizes his gift for poetry and spoken word in the service of creating pertinent dialogue and social consciousness within the grassroots masses.

    At the 2003 Million Youth March he received an award for his support during the movement. He was also featured at the Martin Luther King Jr. labor center for the commemoration of Black liberation army member Safiya Buhkari; as well as Developing Justice Leadership Program-Workshop and Project REAL. As a graduate, he has been instrumental in bringing a positive social message to at-risk youth at local schools, and various social institutions.

    Karast tours various colleges, universities, prisons, homeless shelters, poetry workshops, panel discussions, and community meetings around the country using the microphone as his weapon against oppression. Karast was also a guest on the talk show "The Next Level" hosted by Darlene Brown. He released his first poetry album in 2004 called

"GHETTO SCRIPTURES". His poems were played on 93.5FM radio and 90.3FM radio. Karast's poetry speaks to the crying souls of every ghetto in America, and it was said of him; he is the Tupac Shakur, Marvin Gaye, and Malcolm X of spoken word.

Suicidal Hope

He said if he died and came back to life he'd kill himself again
Said his self esteem was bipolar
So his faith in God became schizophrenic,
Suicidal hood hopes.
Self subjugated expressions
Trapped in a suicide note,
Like Vincent Van Goh.
He said sometimes he would paint
Pictures of the lord lynched in a Michelangelo.
What if god committed suicide?
What if he was Phyllis Hymans depression and overdosed on a love song?
Lithium carbonated induced love songs.
What if he was Curt Cobain's addiction?
What if he was Donnie Hathaway in the ghetto
trying to find his earnest Hemmingway?
Suicidal insanities
Suicidal sons socialized into a psychosis,
No more watching rainbows
Like Ntozake Shange.
For them colored girls who considered
suicide when they should have been watching rainbows.
They say a child is born
Every time a color dies in the rainbow.
Suicidal sacraments
Suicidal rewinds re-enacted thru teenage suicide
Sacrilegious sacrosanct,
Suicidal shadows playing Russian roulette under sycamores,
Suicidal Hope.
He said he saw the world without love so he prayed over the chamber
and put one in his lady.
MAYBE.
If we can see God before the beginning of that noose,
before that pill swallowed becomes an overdose,
before another mother clutches her newborn and bungee jumps with

umbilical cords,
maybe, just maybe Hope wouldn't feel so abandoned.

A Mothers Tribute

Three hundred sixty-five days
Fifty two weeks
Twelve months,
Yet we only give them twenty-four hours,
Flowers devoid of nectar
Appreciations expressed thru half dead roses,
Mother!
What if God had a mother like you?
Would newborns still be abandoned
on the doorsteps of synagogues?
Reverence the womb.
They say heaven lies beneath the foot of our mother's womb,
I Am...
She Is...
Indescribable love expressed thru Hallmarks, Thank You;
Thank You for trying to play a role for a man who never saw me as his own,
For being there when the harsh realities of the hood had me feeling like Sisyphus pushing stones,
Without you a house could never be a home,
Earth could never be the same without the moon,
Underappreciated love.
I wonder if God was a woman
Who created man by swallowing the moon?
If I died and came back to life
I'd be my mother's love reincarnated.
No soul would feel love-less,
No hungry stomachs,
No sunken eyes trying to find

Self identity thru Toni Morrison
Bluest Eyes,
A Mother like you
Tell me, what can be higher than you?
I wonder if the seven wonders of the world had a mother like you.

I Am America

Call me America.
Adopted son of Vespucci,
Born from a conglomerate of thirteen pregnant nuns
Call me your thirteen colonies,
Conceived with a low blood count
So they injected racism in my veins,
From Christopher Columbus to Mark Twain,
From George Washington to senator McCain,
Predicted to rule the world in 1776
So world domination became my savior,
Call me the wolf in shepherd's garb...
Like Klansmen lynching black babies
In a Vatican's garb,
This is America in disguise
Warfare is my Bill of Rights,
Xenophobic by nature so three fifths of a man became clause,
Call me the black man's burden...
Like Aids, like smallpox, like syphilis
Diseases injected into the biology of blackbirds
Conceived with a manifest destiny
So they implanted bow 'n arrows
In my talons,
E-pluribus Unum
Second class citizens from immigrants to coons...WELCOME!
Welcome to a place where western religion is genocide in reverse,

Where patriot acts are training grounds for babies taught how to kill,
Glorify the countries I bombed in my star spangled banners,
Pledge your allegiance...
Pledge your allegiance to the gang violence in my American Flags,
My coat of arms
Justice in America is like a black face in drag.
America!
Land of the enslaved,
Home where the thirteenth Amendment got over 3 Million citizens enslaved,
Tell me...how does it feel
To be just like me?

When I Was A Human Being

I plundered, pillaged, plotted, punished, purged, pummeled, plunged
Looted, lynched, lashed
Lawless liberals like leviathans lewd
Lucifer long tongued
Call My Nature Violent.
Vicious, void, vain, valiant, volatile, venomous
Voraciously, vain-gloriant, vulgar,
Sick souls systematically slaughtered like human sanity.
Slaved, seized, scammed, schemed
Shackled saviors shattered by sanctioned assassinations.
Satanic miscreants.
Macerated massacres maliciously molded like American malfeasance,
Mutilated morals
Maimed, mangled, mocked
Misguided martyrs mimicked like mockingbirds in minstrel.
Call me faceless
Fallible, flatulent, fickle, frolic, flagitious

Fanatics forsaken like faithless theologians.
Tabernacles like taboo
When I was a human being humanity gave me up for an abortion
So all things holy became a taboo,
A theory
A thesis
A tyrannical tear drop war dancing in the winds.
A willows war cry like prison walls,
Warmongering worshippers,
Callous hearts like cell blocks,
Human love handcuffed like chattels in cotton fields,
What is a human being without compassion ?

Read Me A Passage

Call me John the Baptist 10:34
Did I not say in your law
Ye were all gods?
God!
Read me a passage
Like Khalil Gibran philosophizing in the book of prophets,
Like Ibn Maryam chanting Suratal Ikhlas in the book of prophets,
Iqra! Bismi rabbika la thee khalaq,
Read!
Read me a passage.
Hearken to my lamentations
It's like I assassinate myself in every poem.
Call me a suicide writer.
My communion
Drink deeply
Swallow my pain
Let the heavens digest me in her bosom
Dine with me.

Dine with me like the feast of weeks in the book of Leviticus,
My tabernacle.
How many loaves of bread will it take to reach the center of my tabernacle?
My circumference.
Hosea four six,
Verily my people are destroyed because a lack of knowledge in their circumference,
Lay me down in green pastures
Cloak my pain with the same garbs
Gandhi wore around his soul,
My testament.
Read me a couplet.
Pacify the pain in this poem
With a psalm,
Serenity it with a proverb,
Sometimes, it seems like my poems are having nightmares
Like Nebakanezer
Daniel see if you can interpret the dreams in this poem,
Like Annias bless the Saul inside of me with a passage,
Like Arna Bontemps I, too, talk of reapings,
my theology.
Take religion out of man and you'll see every prophet shared the same theology.

Tell My Story

I want yall to tell my story
Tell it.
Let the streets breathe your narrations
Let the seeds germinate
From my rites of passage.
Tell 'em how every poem I wrote was a hidden doorway to another passage.
How I walked backwards on the sands of Sankofa
And had my footprints blessed on the middle passage.
Peruse my Bio.
Tell 'em how long I spent in that cage.
How Dannemora prison torture became the rhythm n blues to the poems I'd carve on the walls/
How Sing Sing tried to crucify my spirits.
How in the solitude of S.H.U. I would cry out to the lord in Aramaic
Maybe that's why I felt abandoned by the lord Attica;
Eli, Eli Eli Lama Sabathani
Tell 'em how shadow boxing prison nightmares had that little boy in me crying out to mommy.
Mommy!
Tell 'em how I would soliloquize with the pain,
Monologue with ice-picks.
Prison riots became my therapy.
Therapeutically, tell 'em how every repetition on the pull up bar became my therapy,
Tell 'em how bipartisan politicians create Frankenstein's out of incarcerated babies.
Patent my visions
Poor man's copyright my poverty in your libraries of congress
And print my hunger in your anthologies
Edit my afflictions
Tell 'em how I was the first born from my old Earth's addiction,

Tell 'em how I saw laughter in affliction
Tell 'em.
Tell 'em how the pain of being a fatherless son caused me to find comfort in Christ's crucifixion.
Rub my forehead in ablutions
Manuscript my scars
Tell 'em to give me three minutes and I'll show the world
Why poets hide their pain behind verses and bars,
Spit it!
Measure my lines in your iambic pentameters and oralize me in your ballots,
Freestyle my destiny with a pilot
Tell 'em how a lost shepherd became a rose.
How I became resurrected in my little brothers suicidal thoughts.
Call me the poet without a soul,
Tell 'em.
Tell 'em every time I write a poem I snatch a part of my life from my soul.
Tell 'em.
Bless my name in two syllables
And call me the greatest poet never told.
Depict my life in a pastoral
And tell 'em.
Just in case I die inside this POEM.

Blind Faith In A Noose

He said every time he reads the bible he sees the devil dancing in minstrel.
Like tea party racism painted in white minstrel,
What if God was an abandoned child without a face?
What if man concocted a virgin birth and made Jesus a conspiracy theory to control your faith?
He said sometimes he would read the bible backwards to see at what point God changed his faith.
What if man created God?
That would explain why women put their faith in man instead of God.
This is blind faith in a noose!
Holy books written by the same theology that held Emmit Tills' noose.
What if mans prayers were assassination attempts on God
Like Michelangelo oil painting spooks,
From slave ships to synagogues,
From slave whips to plantation seminars.
This is blind babes,
pillow cuddling crucifixions,
Like non-believers chanting Allah 31 times in Christian tongues
Fallible tongues
What if god needed an exorcism
What if Jesus' crucifixion was symbolic to humanity in an exorcism,
Like Lauren, what if
Adam did live in theory
Eve, would be an educated guess
A hypothetical thought
Created by immaculate misconceptions,
Like sightless truth
Blind eyes don't see misconceptions,
Sinful births
Sadomasochistic popes creating religious sodomy
And calling it divine truths,
Sins are not rectified in a booth,

The truth.....
What if you woke up and realized you were in someone else's dream
Sleep walking with your eyes wide shut?

She Said I was Too Deep

She said I was too deep.
Your voice should be carved on concrete so the corner stone the builders rejected could feel your passion.
Like Richard King's "Black Dot Black Seed", if poetry was a hidden doorway to the soul then this should be your rites of passage.
Your pantomime reminds me of a Sudanese war child lost in a distorted passage.
Said Jehovah witness the I in me
And compared my canonical gospel to Lazarus,
Said my poetry was like John the Baptist to her River Jordan so she nicknamed me Nazareth.
Call me beautiful mind.
She said if poetry was a Greek tragedy I'd be charged with Socrates' crimes.
Lethal injection by pancuronium bromide.
I said my lady I live in the rain drops.
My mother was heaven and my father was the rainbow
Only came around when I cried.
Call my life an allegory.
Like shadows shackled in Plato's allegory
Allegorically, diagnose me as a paranoid schizophrenic with an insanity to write so it'll be normal when they call me crazy.
Too dichotomic when they call me too deep,
She said, at night she calls the adman and chants Swahili mantras
When her spirits are too confused to sleep,
Trepidated emotions.
Said her selfishness overwhelms her at times so she petitions the Lord to
Re-record my destiny, destiny,

Unlike Herodotus' history is not a lie confirmed.
Its culture lived backwards,
We're living in a backwards culture
Cloned foot prints
Economical recessions got angels and demons walking in the same footprints.
I called her a metaphor.
She called me a simile.
She said, if God is love and love is the union of souls
Then write me a love poem without using metaphors or similes.
I asked her her name she said you can't define me.
I am archetype of humanity
Primeval oceans
Kundalini serpent free versing thru your energy centers
Call me your inner visions.
I exist.
She said, when she called me too deep she just wanted to get into my mind and share my thoughts.

Kill 'Em Before They Grow

Let's kill 'em before they grow.
Cointelpro tactics of ghetto neutralization.
Where justifiable homicide is justified in black faces.
Minstrels painted on pigment-less faces. Attired in black robes got
Americas judicial system looking like Ringling Brothers Barnum and
Baileys in black robes.
Let's kill them before they grow.
Sounds like J. Edgar Hoovers ideology cloned from the grave;
Warmongering xenophobes
Using gunplay dialectics to turn
Ghettos into German warzones
Like Iraq and Iran,
but the square is Congo
and fifty shots to Sean Bell
Remind me of Soweto,
Timothy, little Bobby and Ousmane Zongo, black cops acting like Tonto;
Urban intifadas
I wonder if Cynthia Mckinney knew their names,
If Obama spoke out against police brutality
Or simply tried to Reverend Wright
The wrong from his name,
They say their eyes were watching God,
but what if God was Lucifer in disguise?
Would mark cooper still have thanked his Lord Jesus Christ
for clearing his name?
Let's kill them before grow.
Before panthers start rising from the minds of babes,
and free lunch sessions become preparations for guerilla warfare.
Where for every Sean Bell
there's a D.C. sniper taking aim.
What if, Mein Kampf was actually a code of silence for N.Y.P.Ds?
Would that explain why good cops take the rap for bad names?
Black lives stolen from existence.

Now, I see why virgin mothers are afraid to give birth to gods,
Sometimes, I wish I could look through God's eyes and see why these devils are killing so many lives.
How many shots does it take to kill a rose?

She said His Abuse Felt like God Abandoned Her

She said his abuse felt like God abandoned her
So, to her love has become an atheist.
Heart broken like deferred butterfly wings,
she said every blow felt like a different rhythm in the winds.
Every concussion the bass on a musician's drum.
His touch was like an angry pianist
pressing too harshly on the wrong keys.
Her screams, they sounded like rape victims
writing suicide notes on magnolia leaves.
YES!
I hear the echoes of liquid love in her tear drops.
Her Mississippi River has become like the Titanic.
Temple defiled by sacrilegious insecurities,
Amon Ra no longer illuminates her constellations.
Her moons are like Countee Cullen's Copper suns.
She said her struggles to love another
man was like the re-enactment of a Greek tragedy.
So, she writes in the diary of her past.
History repeated with reincarnated bruises.
Sometimes, she wonders if God was referred to as a woman
would man still domestically abuse his woman,
Wife, mother, aunt, grandmother, great grandmother, sister, daughter,
queen, Nzinga, Hatshepsut, Harriet, Angela, Angelou, Auset, Corretta
King, Shirley Chisolm, Acheapong Nanny, Fannie Lou, Mary Bethune,
Comrade Betty, Comrade Assata, Mother Tee, Mother Tia, Mother Mary,

Mother Mosiah, Mother Earth...
Civilization.
Two hearts ripped apart like African and Asian countries.
Said her love life was like continental drifting.
So she drifts into another realm.

Paranoid

Too schizophrenic to see the image of
God inside another man.
Said God was a backwards thinker
So she referred to all men as dogs.
Yet, she still prays.
More faith based.
Her laughter more jubilant.
Footprints more stalwart.
Too strong to fall weak 'cause now
she has a little girl to raise.

INFINITE

Consider her armed and dangerous with a pen and a vividly intriguing imagination. Infinite was born and raised in Brooklyn, New York. She is a gifted performance actor, choreographer, writer, visual artist and vocalist who often combines her amazing skills with her spoken word performances. It is also a vehicle by which she passionately speaks for her people all over the world.

A graduate of Rutgers University with a Bachelor in Fine Arts (B.F.A.), Infinite has graced stages throughout the East Coast since the delicate age of three. Even then, her destiny was predetermined and her creative passion ignited. Appropriately named Infinite, because of her many indelible talents, she believes the end result of each of her creative endeavors are infinitely unique and thought provoking as well as infinitely rich in creative divinity.

In addition, she is filled with an abundance of natural talent that is waiting to be shared with the rest of the world. It is through these gifts and talents that she believes her work will transcend time allowing her art to continue to educate, nurture, bring hope, revelation, and evoke passion in the lives of others. Whether performing one of her powerfully written poems that identify many of today's social plagues such as racism, socialism, sexism, or through a cleverly crafted and delicately executed choreographed work audiences are guaranteed to be spellbound.

When addressing other topics such as love, intimacy, self-esteem, or male-female relationships Infinite terrifically balances strength with vulnerability that she envelopes in a matter-of-fact delivery. This helps to, naturally draw one into her special world. A world of limitless creativity, not contained within a box, but constructed without walls, ceilings, or windows placed on stage for all to enjoy allowing her to remain infinitely Infinite.

Spoken Word

I don't bring crowds I draw them.
I sketch the lives of Black and Brown faces
on white pages.
So, excuse me if something don't sound quite right.
I write real life and real life don't always sound quite right.

Words stick to my soul like glue traps
and hood rats.
Perhaps I should write my words on glass
so I can watch what I say.
Throw boomerangs with white sheets
so I can learn that my words do come back and haunt me,
and now I must stand behind my words.

So how do you stand behind your words?
Is it like standing behind a shoji?
So we can only see the silhouette
and what will be misinterpreted are
the curves in the vowels.
nOw,
dO mY wOrds tUrn YOU On
or are you just too mesmerized by the sound to listen to the facts?

Like rap,
words revolve as the dj cuts and scratch
Rewinds and pulls it up back.
So that it can repeat
and stick to your soul
Like plastic furniture covers do to skin in summer heat
and with everybody trying to keep cool there's no electricity

So our words no longer hold power
Humans with a god complex
Help us to forget
It is God who really holds the power

broken levees.
Leave many stranded and oppressed.
Fifty shots
with the shooters wearin' the bullet proof vests.

Puts a harder press to the precedent that you are a liability.
So tell me, what does spoken word mean to me?
When actions become its contradiction almost instantly
we act from the words we know in our vocabulary.

So tell me how can some of us ACT in love
when we don't even SPEAK it?
Say things like,
I'm a keep you in my prayers, but you don't really mean it.
See I don't care if you spit sick.
If you're a hypocrite
and rippin' it for you is just a job.

See this is what I live and breathe
and it delivered me
From givin' up and stickin' up
When times got really hard

So, no, I can't afford to do a show for free,
but when I talk to God
He says you're doin' this for Me.
And so, I ACT accordingly.
Cuz this is not just spoken word.

She Gave Life

Step into Motherhood's light.
Bask in the glow that surrounds life.
She is: Friend, Daughter, Sister, Aunt, Niece, Wife.
Let's examine her plight.
Before water breaks
It makes its way through pores as sweat
Makes its way out of eyes as tears
Fears arise and subside all at the same time
Nine months to prepare this eternal contract
Not realizing all you sign away
And all you stand to gain
As contractions become hard to bear
Now, push
Push through the pain
Push because all would stop if you didn't keep going
Push to keep children out of harm's way
Push that one last push to hear the world say
She is
Friend, Daughter, Sister, Aunt, Niece, Wife
and now
Mother
Your personal life guide
You are now her pride
She is your angel with tucked wings
'Cuz she gotta go through some things
which all fall under sacrifice
But she will keep quiet about her struggles
Many hats she will juggle
Rises when all crumbles
To make rubble her stepping stone
Mama we see
And as we grow we watch.
Watch you push.
Because the world would stop if you didn't keep going

Mama we hear
And as we grow we listen
Follow your directions
As you pray every night, we make the right decisions
We are just wishing
We could be a smidgen of the mother you turned out to be
She gave life, but she is the reason why we   live.

Butterfly

Emerged from the cocoon
Before the flowers bloomed
And couldn't survive
Feeble wings try to fly in winter's frost
But gets lost
When all is covered in snow
Take time to grow
That's the cocoon's function
Inside something beautiful is happening
I often wonder if butterflies feel trapped in
Maybe they get impatient too
Or do they understand their destiny
In order to be
What all see as beautiful
They have to go through the ugly
Transform the pain
All the unexplained
Take one stage at a time
It don't last forever
It comes together
And as they pass the paths
Of those
Perceptive enough
To appreciate the plain and pure things
This butterfly will bring

Grace and elegance
to whatever garden
she flies in...
But-her-fly is different
Wings unfold slowly
Flying with changing altitudes
To avoid raindrops
But they fall so numerous
That she must be swift
To avoid getting hit
This creature never intended to roam
Trying to avoid the killer bee's sting
'cuz he's amazed by the color of her wings
Can you blame him?
She's no ordinary butterfly
See-her-fly is different
And you just know
She's okay with flying alone
Her passing reminds you of the beauty
In a weed filled garden
Flowers stand straight
Starving for her attention
But the rain is fallin'
She won't be sidetracked
'cuz-her-fly is different
Amazed by the color of her wings
But does that bring
Faded colors for every flower she encounters?
Or is the flower better
For having met her?
Seeing her?
Maybe she feels ignored
As she flutters by
And she stops
To gain their attention
Perhaps it's to rest
From the stress of traveling alone

Who knows?
But she makes it look easy
Her beauty is her triumph
From the struggles of yesterday
Those days when moving as a caterpillar
Were just too slow for her
But she crept on
Knowing it wouldn't be before long
She became a butterfly

Dandelion

Tingling at cheek
From where fist and face would meet
She was the flower that tried to bloom
Between the cracks in the concrete
As she felt that beat
Pound
Pound
He was the timberland boot that crushed her to the ground
Her lineage of seed
Labeled her a weed
So he felt no need
to treat her like a delicate flower
Dandelion
And as dandy's lying on the ground
Trying to retain her consciousness
He continues to beat
Pound
Pound
Diminishes her of her value and depletes her of her common sense
And as dandy's lying on the ground
She recollects
His vow of holdin' her down
and now

He's holdin' her down
Dandy's lion is treatin' her like prey
Masculine hands
Clenching feminine wrists
She's convinced relationships are supposed to be like this
No bliss
Just fits
Angry hits and kicks
Get ripped from the root
Even when you don't ask for it
See it'll grow right back and when them wounds heal
She'll come right back
Her lineage of seed labeled her a weed
So there was no need
for her to believe
she is a delicate flower
Dandelion
But dandy's lyin' to herself
Despite a pretty exterior
And a classification that can cause her to act inferior
And she's pretending all is fine and dandy
And he can't recognize her real beauty
So he treats her like a weed
He feels no need to treat her like a delicate flower
Dandelion
Holds the hand of a man who will continue to violate
Dandy's messin' around with an African violet
who chooses to be violent, but
suppose she posed as a rose?
Would he show her love and affection that would make her grow?
Or she could stand tall like a daisy
and maybe
He wouldn't persuade
His friends to treat her in a similar fashion
So, that he won't seem crazy
It's crazy the way we
Justify treating people who we think

Don't respect themselves,
but I remember in the garden of life
I was once a dandelion myself
So even though labeled a weed
There is a need to plant the seed of
Delicate flower
'Cuz if you don't
Who will, Dandelion?

Freedom Manifesto

This is for my people caught up in a struggle
I know you're tryin' to fit the pieces in life's puzzle
Where trouble seems to come in triples and doubles
I know you wanna be free
I *know* you want to be free
I'm talkin' 'bout FREEDOM
I'm tellin' you it's free to be dumb
It's free to be dumb
Free
to be
Dumb
Until you realize the cost is great
And you get what you pay for
We've taken the shackles off our feet
To act like freaks in da club
And say we dance
Taken chains off our hands
And placed then around our neck
'Cuz the bigger the chain the more respect
I've noticed that everything looks the same
When there's a glare in your eyes
We've been bling blinded
M.C.'s have turned into M.G.'s
'Cuz now they just MisGuided
Who says the best things in life are free?
It's free to be dumb
Free to be dumb
Free
to be
Dumb
Until you realize the cost is great
You get what you pay for
We need to stop
Turning our corners into modern day auction blocks

Trying to make small change
Being sold for small change
Payin' the big price and getting back
No change
some of us rather die for the street
Than be buried in a book
Would rather do a 5 year bid
Than spend 4 in college
Couldn't pick out a person or point in black history,
But it's to dead gangstas, fictional characters, and celebrities
That they pay homage
Free to be dumb
Free to be dumb
Free to be dumb
Until you realize the cost is great
You get what you pay for
Only time some of us move as a unit
Is when we're doin' the electric slide
We can identify all our wrong,
But some of us are too apathetic to make them right
I remember when all my people used to do was fight
Freedom was worth risking a limb
And even a life
Now it's free to be deaf and not hear the cries
Turn your head to the side
And you won't see
It's free to be blind
Freedom and liberty
Had resulted in imprisonment of the mind
Some of us have hands outstretched
Choosing not to invest
Having no interest
In the things that don't appear as
Propaganda
Blinded by illusions
Deaf to the truth

Social and spiritual sore throats
Got the majority mute
Just look all around you
Things have to fall in our laps
For us to touch and taste the proof
Then when the smoke is clearing
There's nothing left but an excuse
The quality of soil in which you sew
Will reap the same quality fruit
So we deduce
There is no freedom
Just fee-dom
You get what you pay for
Inflation says you pay more
And money talks in basic vocabulary
Thank You, please, and, gimme
With little in return
Now, you get what you pay for
Used to be you get what you earned
When will some of us learn?
Well, some of us won't
Education is too expensive
And when FREE is all you have as tender
You just surrender.

J. Steven Williams aka "Tha Real"

Raw and gritty like the sand. This analogy can be used to describe this particular poet. Tha Real entered the world of spoken word after members of a theater group consisting of poets, singers, models, and actors reached out to him to form "The Production. Tha Supa Group". During this time he wrote and memorized his first poem "They" and was encouraged by his comrades to build on his craft.

While living in a New York City shelter he wrote poems as an alternative to succumbing to his circumstances. With three more poems written, "Mellow", one of the members of the group suggested that he try performing in front of a live audience. Tha Real's poetic debut garnered him a cash prize.

In 2010, Tha Real formed a poetic collective called Untamed Talent with the purpose of exposing the world to quality and unadulterated spoken word art form.

The Real has performed at various venues such as the Nuyorican Poets Café, where he also won a prize for his talent. At Medgar Evers he offered his talents in a benefit to help the people of Haiti. Youth Speaks, an event put together by Nicole Bell, the wife of Sean Bell who was murdered by New York City Police Officers he was a featured artist.

Tha Real also tried his hand at producing a show called The Truth Speakers Project: A spoken word open mic with a family feel and is both poetry and audience friendly.

If you asked him what is his brand of poetry, after telling you "real" he would then say his approach to spoken word is "Left-Handed Thinking". As someone who is actually left-handed he does a lot of things differently than many other people; from ironing to cooking, but it's never more obvious than in his poetry.

If he's not finding a new way to look at the N-word, or writing about ills of his community he writes poems like "Hate", which takes a humorous, but serious look at issues as small as riding on the train to as serious as parenting skills.

"I know the power of my words, I know the power of poetry. Combine that with an addiction for creation and performing…yea yall better get used to me…Imma be here for a while" -Tha Real

Better Than Me

When I look at you I see your mother
That is until I move
'Cause when I move, you move
Yea just like that.
Walkin', talkin', just like me
Even got a lil' pot belly just like me
But let me say it from now
I want you to be better than me

I am not saying I was that bad
I mean there are some qualities I possess
Every man wishes he had
But there are some kinks in my armor
And if you don't believe me
Just ask ya momma

I'm sure that she would attest
If you take away my short comings
I was by far the best

Be a man of your word
It's more important than you will ever know
But keep your words to a minimum
Let your actions be what they respect and know

Never take advantage of the weak
Because the strong lose power everyday
And one day someone will shit on you
And "that's what you get" will be what most people will say

Never play with a woman's heart
Because if she gives it to you
She has given you all of her

And sooner or later after so many fuck ups
Your luck will run out
Leaving you missing all of her.

Never do anything if you don't give it your all
You're blessed to be the best
And the others will pray and pray for your downfall

So make 'em hate how bright you shine
But respect your grind
But you gotta stay humble no matter what
Bottom line.
'Cause once you get cocky
Trust me you get sloppy
You won't be able to see your enemies
Creepin up behind
I bet that was the 2nd to last thing to race threw Tony Montana's mind

Learn from your mistakes
Not just how to get around it next time
But learn and understand the reaction to your actions
That way doing the right thing will stay on your mind

You're gonna slip
You're gonna fall
You're gonna cry
You're gonna hurt

Go through it and get over it quickly
Because if you don't
You might get stuck on the island of self pity

Now you have the blue print
The same one I wish my father would have given me
But, then again, I'm not like him
But you are like me.

So remember Malik
If it's up to me
You will be all I am and more
Yes, my son, you will be better than me.

Collateral Damage

What does the truth look like to someone who's never seen it?
How does love sound when it's been said, but they never mean it?
Emotionally, she switched lanes without even signaling
Never looking in her rear view
Jaded and emotionally faded
So many reasons why love and her never made it
Feeling like that person running late for the train and never made it
Her heart and soul battered and bruised
Tired of her feelings and pleasure box being used
She has decided she will strike first and hard
From here on
It's the man who will be the one wearing the scars
She developed an appetite for emotional destruction
Any sign of verbal altercation
She gets to verbally dumping
'Cause saying "I don't need you" is nothing
She loves to see the men crumble from the inside
Getting nourishment from the tears that men cry
Because to her emotional carnage
Is a Picasso
A Van Gogh
A Martin Scorsese flick
She saves the goodfellas for last
Because she say they taste the best
And to think only one man created this mess
Because it was her love
Her love yea
Her L.O.V.E.

Her **L**egs **O**pen **V**ery **E**asy
That helped make her so beastly
Momma never told her 'bout them male predators
The ones who see all females as filthy slut whores
So one day in the wrong place
At the right time
She was hit
Never fully recovered
To busy jumping in and out of covers
With people that outside she cried

Oh please that's my brother
But what no one seen was her inner cry
The pain on the inside
That she pushed way down inside
And covered it up with false pride
Because she never really knew what real love felt like on the inside...

IGNORANCE

I just wanna take this time to thank of all of you for who I am.
WHO AM I?
I am what tells you weed is a good thing.
I am what tells young black men "If you can't find a job, find a drug, a corner, and slang."
I am the mentality of men who feel when it comes to women "If you can't shut'em up then beat'em up."
I am the mentality behind those who think a prison record represents being gansta or keeping it real.
I am that cop from the suburbs who works in the city and thinks every city kid is a drug dealer or potential stick up kid.
I am the mentality behind those people who know any and everything about HIV/AIDS and still "shoot up", have unprotected sex, and then act surprised when they contract the virus.
I am the mentality of that pregnant woman who still drinks, smokes cigarettes or weed, and missed doctor's appointments and then wonder why her baby has a low birth weight and can't come home.
I am the mentality of those who rape, kill, and discriminate against those who don't look like me, think like me, come from where I come from, or tries to date one of my kind.
I am that shot from that gun to get respect.
I am that buck-fifty (150 stitches) that blood left across that old lady's neck.
I am the root to broken homes due to cheating
And the behavior disorders of over and under eating.
I am the reason that blacks and Hispanics are the majority, but are always treated like the minority.
I am those men and women who think what makes a man is the size of his magic stick
And the reason why black men only go to the doctor when they really, really feel sick.

I am the mentality of that single mother who goes back and forth to court for child support thinking she's making him pay when all she gets in the end is $50 every Tuesday and he's still not there to be a father anyway.
I am that woman who tries to hide the black eyes and justifies the black eyes with "He does it because he loves me."
I am that man or woman that finds it in their heart to forget when a loved one has cheated, but never learned to forgive.
I am the homeless who say the streets, compared to a city shelter, are a better place to live.
I am HATE, ANGER, MISTRUST, CONCEIT, FALSE PRIDE and most of all FEAR.
I...AM...IGNORANCE...and I will never die.

Mis-Praise of Man

WHAT? Are you crazy?
Me, not a man?
With all the stuff I do.
I pay all the bills in my house.
I go to work every day.
I give my wife money every payday.
I make sure my kids want for nothing.
I take my family out at least twice a month.
I've never cheated on my wife.
I come home every night.
I make sure my family's needs are taken care of before mine.
I make sure every time me and my wife make love she is satisfied.
I take care of all my responsibilities.
BUT ISN'T THAT WHAT A MAN IS SUPPOSED TO DO?

Right Here

Right now, at this moment
Someone is being raped
Someone is hungry
Someone is badly sick
Someone is being infected with HIV, Hepatitis C., or some crazy STD
Someone is committing suicide
Someone's mother just died
Some kids are left to fend for self—all alone
Someone just heard a loved one die on the phone
DAMN. WHERE AT?
RIGHT HERE.
WHERE?
RIGHT HERE.
Every day and night I hear
'Bout things goin' on elsewhere
But what about the things goin' on here
Where?
Here. Right here.
OPRAH made a lot of noise
When she went to Africa and built those schools
And helped all the poor lil' girls and boys
Man, please kill that noise
How many schools in The Chi, The Stuy, and the Heights did she pass?
And I'm supposed to support her? She can kiss my entire ass?
Brad and Angelina wanted to look a lil' bigga
So they imported some instant clout
A lil' Chinese baby and of course the classic lil nappy head nigga
Get the hell outta here!
I know at least 15 kids, personally, in foster care—they need too.
Should they go to Africa and get adopted by some celebrity just to be treated good here.
No, I'm seriously asking you.

She Try (Housewife Blues)

From making new outfits
Out of what fits
She try

From making sure the kids eat
To making sure birthdays and Christmas
Are always sweet
She try

She try, she try.
Day in, day out
You wanna know what she's about
Just look at the frustration in her eyes

'Cause she try. She try.
Tries to take care for the kids
Making sure they got a place to live
Making sure her man always come home
Because it's too easy for him to roam

She try. She try.
DAMN. SHE TRY.

Most times her frustration comes off
As her being a bitch
But how pleasant would you be
If you spent every day you see,
Lookin' at the same four walls
And taking care of the babies
From feedin' them to hand washing their draws

Lawd, OH LAWD JUST GIVE HER A BREAK!

Thank You
(Dedicated to Gwendolyn Williams)

You nursed me when I was sick.
You fought for me when I couldn't
When I cried, it was you who wiped the tears.
When I was scared, it was you who faced my fears.
Many times, you sacrificed many things for me.
From money to food, and even your own happiness at times.
All just to see a smile on my face.
You even put your freedom on the line
to make sure I had what I needed.
And when I was at the end of my rope
you gave me some of yours.,
All in the name of support.
From my very first time,
To realizing what I wanted to be in life,
You had my back.
Because of that,
And everything above
I just wanna say "Thank you, Momma"
From your son, with nothing, but love.
Just a day or two
For her to do all the things she wanna do
Without having to wash someone else
Dress someone else
Sometime for her to just sit in the damn bathroom by herself.
Even if all she do is cry.
'Cause she needs to vent alone from being all alone.
No one ever hears her cry.
Too busy depending on her, needing from her
But it's hard to get anything in return for her,
But baby I'm tellin' you
Don't cry. Please dry your eyes.
'Cause I know...Trust me I know

That all you do is try.
And I am so proud of you.

The Search

I must have heard this line
A thousand times,
That a good man is hard to find.
Well my question to you is "Where have you looked?"
'Cause you're not gonna find him in a "Terry McMillan" book.
"They're married, locked-up, or gay."
Well, I'm sorry you feel that way.
'Cause I see good brothers every day.
Some are doctors and lawyers. Yeah ,that's true,
but they're also single fathers, construction workers, and job searchers too.
Some of them are going through a lot
And really need that right woman to fill that lonely spot,
But if all you look at is the car he drives, or the money he makes,
Then you will continue to only find,
What is truly, truly fake.
And if that's what you use to judge a good man
You'll always miss the mark.
'Cause in order to find a good man, you must first look at his heart.
I've heard that "All men are dogs",
And that might be true,
Cause just like there are dogs that will hurt you,
There are dogs that are loyal, and will protect you too.

They

They say: "It takes an entire village to raise a child."
Well, if that's true, then someone needs to tell the village, that our crops are going wild.

They say: "The children are the future",
but what kind of future can they be, when so many of our so called futures, are laid to rest and placed behind bars every day.

They say: "Knowledge is power."
Well, I guess that's why we got so many security guards, at dead end jobs.
Making $5.15 an hour with bachelor's degrees.

They say: "Mama's baby, Daddy's maybe."
Well, if that's true then why should daddy stick around?

They say: "All men are dogs."
Which makes all women cats, and cats are far sneakier than dogs.,
So who could really not be trusted?

They say: "A man curses 'cause he doesn't know what to say",
but sometimes you gotta say f*** it.

They say: "The cops are your friend and are here to serve",
but I never heard of anyone ordering 41 bullets.

They say: "Never let your right hand…know what your left hand is doing."
What the hell does that mean?

They say: "Good thing comes to those who wait",
but they never tell you how long you gotta wait.

So, you know what I say about THEY.
Forget 'em, because if THEY

Spent less time being THEY
And more time being US
 Then WE would be alright
And if THEY hear this and get offended too bad
Because you know what THEY say:
"YOU CAN'T PLEASE EVERYBODY ALL THE TIME."

When I Push Out

When I push out I don't want no one to shed a tear,
Pour out some liquor or even share a beer.
Why?
Because if you knew me
You know this was not my speed.
If you knew me
You know I was about laughter,
great sex, real talk and some good w***.
When I push out just know it was not a mistake
My higher power saw I was tired and called me home
for my break.
When I push out don't look for any funeral or wake
'cause when I was alive.
I never wanted to be around that many people
Whose words were far from genuine and closer to fake.
When I push out don't just speak about all the good or the bad.
Mix it up 'cause I lived like that.
So, it can't be all happy and sho nuff not all sad.
When I push out think of me for more than my jokes and temper.
I had a loving heart damn it. I hope someone will remember
I loved hard, cared harder, and many times could have been a ruthless
dude, but never bothered.
And to all people I may have done wrong,
What can I say now? Nothing. I'm gone.

Trevis Moore

The early part of Trevis Moore's life he grew up on the rough streets of Fort Pierce, Florida. Coming to Brooklyn, New York at age 15 he was lured by the idea of becoming "The Man". It wasn't long before Trevis found himself incarcerated, looking at a fifteen to twenty-five year sentence.

Trevis entered prison with very limited reading or writing skills. His knowledge of the streets and constant anger was all he had to protect himself while serving time. Upon learning of the death of his grandmother, Trevis' life took a drastic turn. In his frustration of not being able to write his grandmother a letter before her death, Trevis was moved to work on an area of deficiency in his life. He began to read more while working on writing as much as possible.

The result was the birth of an author. Trevis became a ghostwriter for many of the other prisoners who needed someone to put their words on paper. During twenty-five years of imprisonment, Trevis allowed his pen to show off the dormant talents that were awakened.

His writing skills came from time spent reading everything from Science Fiction greats like Isaac Asimov and Gene Rodenberry to Urban Literature authors such as Iceberg Slim and Donald Goines. Trevis developed a unique writing voice that gave birth to a new genre: Urban Science Fiction; a blend of the hard streets with the "what if?" factors of Science Fiction.

My Love Takes Flight

My love takes flight
Day after Day
Night after night
It soars to the highest heights
Looking for a heart to call home
For far too long it has wandered and roam

My love takes flight
Its lived in cold stone
Slept in a bed of thorns
Been used as a pin cushion
Mistaken for a crook
Sung about
Talked about in books
Caught on good looks
Used as a rook
Burned
Overcooked

Again, tonight
My love takes flight
To search and seek
A place to rest its feet
And drink something sweet
Looking for a retreat
Help me please
Take this rib so I may live

My love takes flight
I guess it's going to be another long night
Need somebody to get my back
Longing for that beacon
That shining light

A space that's tight
Come fly with me
Set me free

My love takes flight
Day after day
Night after night.

A Poem To The Unborn (BLACK SEED)

(Black seed) Dear child,
First things, first.
Do not believe in the curse
Noah is not your granddaddy
Know this is my child
That you are coming from a place that's far beyond
Our people are children of the sun
So you see when you get here you'll be strong
And you'll grow to have limbs that's long
Eye's the same color as a lion
Skin like sugar unrefined
With a mind as sharp as a thin line
And have a black man's piece of worldly pride,
But don't worry I won't name you Leroy or Clyde

(BLACK SEED)
Son you are going to need some survivor tools.
So, while you rest in the testes I will take you to school,
And to teach you this lesson I will put this in the form of rules.
#1. Grow to be a man. One who understands that he's God's plan.
#2. Be smarter then. Each and every man be a rocket ship. Don't ever land.
#3. Be free. Son they are going to try to hold you and try to teach you not to love you. Embrace their religion and be a member of one of their prisons.
#4. Be aware of those that look like you. Many are agents for the ruling reign. Somehow those @$#$%^& got into their brain.
To them killing you wouldn't be a thing.
There are those who are just man in a frame,
but beneath they are strange.
Liking to touch little boy's wee-wee
If a buster try this you come tell me.
#5. Black on black love is good. Yes, I know what I said up there. That's for those fools who act like they're on that rock. Don't worry they are.

Easy to spot
when they are in groups.
They make it hot
 High school drops, most.
Without their pops.
 Nevertheless, that's just the few don't let it turn you blue.
'Cause you learn to save your love
For those who are true and when you do
Pour on the love like it's that Gorilla Glue
Especially for the old and the new

(BLACK SEED)
Yes, son I know that you are ready to make the trip.
Hoping I hurry up and find you a ship
Say when you get here you're going to flip the script.
Be the new improved Hannibal
You want to be named Malcolm next
See yourself as Huey P. on parade.
Rest boy. Just relax.
You're going to have plenty time to knock suckers on their back.
Oh and remind me to get you a vest and mack
'Cause I see you're not going to give any slack.

Well, for now that's that.
Yeah, I'm coming right back.
Someone's knocking on the doors of my mind and I got to find out who's that.
Ok, ok. I'll work on getting you here today.
It's this thin piece of rubber that's causing the delay.

Says warning if taken off.
I will have to pay.
Yes, child let us pray.
Your ship will come one day.
While you're waiting read my DNA.
Keep to your studies
Stay away from the strays

'Cause they're only going to be around a couple days
Ok peace and be brave.
Stay hid in your little cage until you are paged.
Keep running and exercising 'cause it going to be a long race.
You've got to stay in front of the waste to get first place.
This is where you pick your mother.
So, you got to outrun the others.
Ok, go ahead and get some rest.
While I survive this mess.
Got to chase these checks.
Peace and God Bless
Black Seed.

Mr. Right?(Can I Get A Cup Of Sugar?)

Hello, Miss. My name is Mr. Right.
I live around the corner of Goodbrother Street
I was wondering if I could borrow a cup of sugar?
I asked the lady across the street. She only had pepper. Her sister offered me salt.
The one down the block tried to feed me pork.
The sista next door is taking me to court.
All I need is a cup of sugar, but every time I say my name they start acting strange.
Out comes the handcuffs and chains.
Voices change
I feel like I'm surrounded by G.I. Jane
And most don't believe that Mr. Right is my name 'cause they always sat no you're not.
Miss, really, I am. Just ask my mother and pastor,
But don't ask my brother, Mr. Wrong 'cause he's going to lie and say that he's Mr. Right and try to fee you bull----.
Please, get you home to his solid gold dog bone
One I suggest you leave lone.

You should run when you see him coming.
and don't ask my sista Ms. Wrong
'cause she still licking her wounds.
She and Mr. Wrong got into a fight.
He hit her with a pipe.
That put out her lights.
Ever since, she hasn't been right
In the head
And something in her heart done went dead
Her eyes are always red
She'll lie and say that I am
Mr. Scared To Commit
That I think I'm the S@#T
Like to hit and quit
Got a lot of women
No none of this is true
She just down and blue
So, can I get that cup of sugar?
Ana a little bit of milk
Oh, you too? Don't believe that that's my name. Such a shame
That all you got is a little bit pepper and table salt
That you are about to put on some pork
 After that you're on your way to court
So, what's up with that handcuffs and chains?
What's your name?
G.I. Jane
Damn
Hello, Miss
My name is Mr. Right
I live around the corner of Goodbrother Street
I was wondering if I could borrow a cup of sugar?

Old Friends

Hey my brotha
My sista
Do you remember me from back in the day?
The fun we had when we use to play
At your house or mine
There was a place at the table
House full because we were the only ones with cable
The old folks in the hood kept us stable
The black church gave us the good kids label
Old friends
You were my first love
My first kiss
I'm sorry that life gave itself a twist
And add a long list,
But you are the one I miss the most
Breakfast in bed
Eggs and toast
Heard that you got three and are expecting one more
I wish they had been mine
Nevertheless, I hope you are doing fine
Anyway, give me call
I'M SORRY THAT LIFE GAVE ITSELF A TWIST
Drop a line from time to time
I just wanted to let you know that you are on my mind
I miss you and I'm not lying
Old friends
Is that bullet for me?
Gee, have you forgotten when we use to smoke the tree?
The only way you can love me if I'm six feet deep
This over a woman or the street
What happened to the days of black love, black pride, black family?

My homie
My one and only
We are friends, right?
Remember hanging under the street light all night?
You had that dog named Duke
And my grandmother had that crazy cat
Old man Smitty lived in the back
Remember how we use to pull trains on Pat?
Man she grew up to be alright
I even made her my wife
Old friends
We made it just like we planned
Now, we got to reach back
And help our friends
Be the 2011 Robin Hood or the modern day Peter Pan
Protect the babies for they will be the next man and woman
Understand that this isn't a matter of skin 'cause color don't pick your friends
Old friends
It's sad that we have blown to the four winds
Not knowing when we will see each other again,
But like old lace is our friendship
it's there preserved in its special place
You are in my heart like blood
Old friends
Please come again
and let us
The precious memories

Brotha Man

Man, it's impossible for black men to be so lame
Hey, bro don't you recognize me?
It's your brotha man
I mean, sure, I could use a lil' tan
Man, why are we fighting again?
Oh, it's our fifth bottle of gin
That's when killing each other stopped being a sin
You'll put my lights out over ten
Dude, we know each other
Mama and them
Hey, brotha man
living in this world is a struggle for me to
and just like you
I got beef with the boys in blue
I got problems getting a job
and because I don't have a fancy car
from the chicks I get snobs
No, that wasn't me who robbed.
No, I'm not trying to play hard
Bro, put away the gun
Now, what's that going to solve?
Lets talk like men
Act like we some kin
They had stud farms back when
to increase the slave population
Today we would all be on Maury
Mr. Shaka are you our father?
I ask because we are such warriors
Brotha man don't give my sista the AIDS
unless you are going to raise her three children
You are suppose to be willing to kill for them
not kill them yourself

Cover your dirty staff
or on judgment day feel the wrath
Brotha man, let us reason
Let us stop this treason
of our nation
Times a wasting
we're stuck on repairs
while everybody else is racing
Black man awaken
Let's get it shaking
and baking
Get back to our place, kings
Brotha man, can I come out to tonight?
Please, no shots tonight
Brotha man
Hey, Mr. President
How is all that money spent?
Can you see me?
'Cause I know you sit behind all that tin
Bro, we need some jobs and sh--
Here's our list
Yeah, yeah get back with us on this
Brotha man, peace

Yes, I Am back

If you are calling me a pen monster
Yes, you are right
Yes, I am a poet for life
Yes, each line is tight
Yes, I'll still be at it at first light
Yes, I am getting ready to take flight
So, hold on tight
I've been eating strictly rice
So that I'm poet test ready
Take ten steps and let you have it
Yes, I think I'm the sh--
About to call up Ms. Late Nite. Maybe she'll let me hit
Yes, this is fresh
Off of the dome
It's third and fifteen and
I'm about to go long
in the name of Kush
I done donated a lung
Yes, I do this for fun
Remember when I wrote "My Plasms"
You know I only drop bombs
So much heat I set off alarms
Such a writer
 I got inky palms
and permanent dents
in my forefinger and thumb
Yes, our situation got me stress
Got sh-- on my mind that I need to get off my chest
Yes, I want to go out on a date
Baby, I can't afford the restaurant just get you a plate
Yes, I hate when the cab keep going and make me late
Yes, I love my mother
Yes, we shall overcome
Yes, I'm going to keep going

'Cause I be knowing
I'm pregnant
Is my stomach showing?
Yes, I'm still growing
The call to war
I am going to keep blowing
The ninth ending
we're down a couple runs
Time for us to get to scoring
Let the lyrics start pouring
Get the love flowing
Brothas and sistas
writing a million poems
Yes, I am God's son
You may breathe now
My gas has passed
Attention
Yes, soldier the general is done
No, you may not pick me out a wife
Hey, would you like a bowl of rice.

Ms. Love Me

Hello, hello?
Is this mic on?
Ok, ok
I got something to say
Today, I feel like singing
"Oh, happy day".
Will you look at the sun's rays?
She is so beautiful, I'm amazed.
Shine so bright that I got to wear shades.
Please, forgive me 'cause I'm really not a holy roller, but just this once
I want to say, glory hallelujah.
Man, you would too.
If you only knew
things she does to
my heart and soul.
Without her in this world
it would be so cold.
When she calls I never keep her on hold.
I am helpless when her perfume hits my nose.
The color of a black rose.
Mahogany and gold.
The mother of my prose.
Just one touch and there he blows.
This is unexplainable, but anybody who's been in love before knows
how this goes or, at least, I suppose.
They do, oh, my queen
it is from God which you came.
Just as Sheba traveled the desert to reach Solomon
I wish I could give you one of the rings around Saturn
with Venus as a stone.
So unyielding and strong
Ms. Love Me you helped me get up on my word game.
Told me to try picturing life frame by frame.

And that if I get a little rough sometimes
don't be ashamed.
Thank you love for you have been with me through many pages.
My literary rages.
The key to my mental cage.
It's because of your patience.
That I have walked across stages
to standing ovations.
Ms. Love Me you are my puff puff pass.
If the other woman in my life knew how much I love you
she'd be mad.
So, I keep our love affair on the stash.
How do you like your new pad I bought you?
Yes, it's empty, but let's see what we can do.
To make it a home
how about writing poems all over its walls?
Doors and windows and spill ink all over its floors.
Paint it black and blue.
Let's get started because its got so many rooms.
Ms. Love Me, thanks for being my lover and friend.
For being here when times are good and bad
happy and sad.
With you I am never alone.
Ms. Love Me, God knows man is as old as the sands
and that lust is the most joyful of sins.
I am Superman when you're in my hand.
 You got me catching bullets, stopping trains and want to know what's my name? What's my name?
Ms. Pen! Ms. Pen!
Ms. Love Me!
Ms. Love Me set me free.
Such a sweet release
don't you agree.

CUPID

Cupid! Hey, man!
What did I tell you about playing?
Look, fool, you done shot me again.
And here I was thinking you were my friend.
Didn't I tell you after the last OOPs! I was going to kick your—
Child, you and that damn toy. Why couldn't you a normal little boy and pick a nice little red car?
And look what you did to those birds, man. You have people running scared.
To some love is the most evil word they've ever heard.
Take Samson, for example. The shot you gave him made his brain scramble.
You done left some lives in shambles.
And some, like me, have been shot with more than just one of your arrows.
I've been shot so many times love is in my bone marrow.
I'm so full I can sell it by the barrel.
Thanks to you I got it in favors.
Bitter and sweet.
I can't measure it cause it's too deep.
Boy you damn near made me take a few leaps.
Had me thinking about jumping 'cause I almost confused love with humping.
Why do it keep feeling like I done broke something.
And what's causing my throat keep lumping.
Can't remember if my name is Trevis, Baby, or Pumpkin
Boy! Son, you done did it this time.
Done crossed the line.
Your poison done entered my mind.
Now, I see that love is deaf dumb and blind.
And should be served with a slice of lime.
Young man this is a crime.
Who, me? I'm doing just fine.

It hurts, but I am far from dying.
He who say he has never loved before is lying.
Ok, then why are you crying.
Well, here I am again at loves starting line.
Or is it hate?
Wait.
Was that an earthquake?
Does the heart taste good with shake and bake
I'm not a vampire so what's up with the stake.
I heard you could buy love for a good rate.
Cupid my boy you're still a baby. So, what do you know?
You just go around shooting people with your bow and arrow.
Did you know that the line between love and hate is thin and narrow.
That is ground some like an airplane and make others soar like a sparrow.
Was it love or hate that brought down the towers?
Anyway don't shoot me again my friend or our relationship must end.
'Cause my heart has been broken so many times it's starting to turn to sand.
So you go and play and try not to hit me with any strays for at least a couple of days.
Run alone and find the lonely.
Those who are looking for their one and only.
Boy, don't you point that arrow at me!

THE

The way she flows is so new to me.
The tingle I feel feels good to me.
The dream. Could this be the key to set me free?
The end to the silent screams.
The brain's pain reliever.
The deep, deeper, the deepest.
The queen on the chessboard of my life for that she got to be nice.
Able to sustain on a daily grain of rice.
The price? The hearts locking device.
The flesh. The bone.
The one who makes me leave my father's home.
The reason why this thing grows hard and long.
The reason for the word home.
The sexy and grown.
The grey poupon.
The explosion. That thing is the bomb.
The calm.
The one on my ark.
The great white in my ocean.
The twin to my motion.
The #5 love potion love.
The world to me.
The #2 bringer of #3; be it he or she.
The fertile crescent.
The herbal essences.
The chocolate in my kisses.
The who you the brand to the new.
The sky when it's blue.
The connection to you.
The wedding suit and shoes.
The, the, the, "the"
Sista. Mother. Friend.
The beginning.
The end.

Don't It Hurt?

Don't it hurt when you feel stuck in a groove and you can't move?
How about when you can't afford to buy the food you choose or buy your child new clothes and a good pair of shoes?
Don't this type of stuff make you cry the blues?
Don't it hurt when you need something fixed, but don't have the tools?
Don't it hurt when you know you should be driving, but you just keep on walking?
Don't it hurt when you're locked in a cage; just you and your rage?
How about when you're in your lonely room and the shadows rule?
Your Mama's baby, but your daddy's name is, Who?
Does life make you ask Alex, "Can I get a clue?"
Don't it hurt when you can't say no when you know that's the answer you should give?
Don't it hurt when you got 25 to life for something you didn't do and you just lost your last appeal?
For this, would you kill for the executioner? Is this enough to kill?
Don't it hurt when you are sick, but don't have the money to pay the bill?
Don't it hurt when you know that you are a giant, but you're treated like a midget?
 Don't it hurt when the other man got the nerve to exalt himself over you?
Hey, I mean what can you do when they don't have a clue?
We know that from darkness the world grew.
From a black dot all other colors became new.
That includes white, brown, gray, and blue.
This is called hue-man. Can you understand?
Don't it hurt when you watch the North and South poles melt away 'cause you know that they are what keeps this ship from floating away from its docking bay.
Don't it hurt when you know that you are in the matrix and you done picked the wrong damn pill ?
Yo, man!
Give a brother a second shot.
I'll make you a sequel unequal to none.

The mental hot desert sands.
 I've run out of my cocoon. I don't butterfly'd.
Can't you see me looking pretty?
Man they can't touch me.
I'm mentally nasty.
I got the codes, see?
Don't it hurt when love hurts?
Now, what exactly is that?
What if love isn't on your emotional soundtrack or you want to love, but something keep holding you back?
Ok, how many vowels do I get 'cause to women I don't seem to be saying the right things?
I keep trying to tell them where the key to my heart is.
A few have come close, but all have fell in love's ditch.
Some just missed.
Got on the wall and slipped.
From them, not one tear dripped.
Ladies, please shut your bottom lip.
A Salute goes out to Solo-mon.
Don't it hurt when you know that your paycheck is gone before you get it?
I could go on for days with the pain and shame, but it hurt too much.
Don't it hurt!

SHE

She is the first mother.
The life-bringer to all others.
See, Dude since we all bleed that makes us brothers.
Every woman on this planet the second mother.
I mean, man, she's like no other.
Come in such array of colors.
Love her in that chocolate, coconut, almond, and caramel covered.
Look how she gleam when my daddy hit her with the hot beam.
Such nice mountains and peaks.
 Antarctica cools her feet.
Her hair is the color of wheat.
She uses the Sahara as a bed when she sleeps.
Baked a dark brown from the heat.
Her skin goes from chalk to Indian ink.
Her twin chocolate kisses are so sweet.
Her voice blows thought me like a gentle summer breeze.
She's so green. Look at those trees.
You make breathing so neat.
I swear I can feel your every move when I sleep.
She brings forth fruit from my tree.
That is unless I get her pee'd! Then she strips me like Jesus.
Did the fig tree hit me with a North pole freeze?
Baby, please.
Can't you see me on my knees?
She covers me with her summer rain.
I found my fountain of youth in the gushers from her hot spring.
Isn't it a shame that she takes men's needles deep in her veins?
She rejuvenates me when she lets me dip in the pool at the end of her valley so deep.
She's a breath of fresh air to my every day.
Holder of my sunray.
Most Beautiful vision when I blaze.
She can go postal, hit me with a pot of hot oatmeal, go into a rage,
Take over the front page as a category five and wash me away like in a mudslide

If I get on her wrong side.
Be careful to pay attention her tides.
I love when she gets fly.
Rocks so many diamonds you can see them from the sky.
She...

Empress Poetry

Empress Poetry is the author of Impressions of a Poet, Footnotes of my Journey; Co-host of Three Ingredients One Foundation, an internet radio show; Co-Founder of Urban Trilogy, Poet, Performer, Mentor, Mother and daughter of the Most High.

Born on the beautiful island of Barbados, living in New York City, Empress Poetry has embraced her responsibility as an ambassador of Spoken Word. She uses her talents to empower, inspire and edu-tain. She acknowledges her God given talents and vows to use it for good, so she mentors teen girls in High Schools and lends her voice for fundraisers and community service.

She encourages others to tap into their word power and use it to benefit themselves and others. Empress loves poetry. Empress is POETRY!

Come Meet a Man

Come meet a man who has made promises I know that he will keep.
A man who looked into my soul, deep.
Saw my wounds and healed me.
A man who will not deceive me.
He loves me from my hair follicles to my toenails.
Told me if I trust in Him; I would never fail
Come meet this man.
Come meet a man who met me when I was down.
I had nothing and no one.
My smile was really a frown.
Come meet this man who loves me for me.
Has opened my eyes and allowed me to see.
LIFE!
Not just any life, but a life of my own.
A life where there is progress and I can see my growth.
A life where He is my guidance, my protector, my friend.
A life that when it's over I'll look forward to the end.
Come meet this man.

Who I Am

He asked me, who do you think you are?
I paused for a moment and this poem came to mind.
I am a daughter of the Most High.
Mother of all Mankind.
I am a woman designed with a purpose.
A purpose she strives to exemplify.
I've borne doctors and lawyers and presidents.
Raised athletes and scholars of dance.
I've inspired young queens to rise and claim their queendoms.
And encouraged young kings to pull up their pants.
I was created to leave a footprint on this world.
I am every little girl playing mother.
Every 13-year-old dreaming of her future lover.
The children, the cars and the fence.
Every 16-year-old that's tried to figure out what the word love meant.
I am that 18-year-old young lady graduating to another stage.
That 21-year-old with her ambitions all in a rage.
I am that 22-year-old mother raising her child in un-chartered waters without a father.
Making me that broken spirited sister.
The one that you call bitter.
The one who is begging you to look past her face,
Look into her eyes, see her future.
To see if you find your place.
And if you don't , then please leave.
See, being a single mother did not kill my dreams.
My daughter makes me dream my dreams into reality.
Being assigned to her, made me examine me.
Forced me to embrace my destiny
and brought me closer to God.
Who I, now, know carries me over the rocky roads.
He gives me the strength needed for me to carry my load.
Cocooned me as I experienced my transformation.
His Word nurtures my inspiration and I've emerged the Empress I am

today.
There is so much more to say,
but I'd rather show you.
Show you what my future holds and if it's something you're not into
then I would have to show you the door.
See, time for games, I have no more.
Since I've discovered my destination
I'm paving the way to help strengthen our nation.
To heal the broken, build bridges, to find common ground.
To start rebuilding a foundation that was once sound.
I ask you, are you the one assigned to take this journey with me?
The king I will stand with and support as he leads?
The one determined to mend our family?
Are you a man of His Word?
Because that's who I will need as I mature into that 40-year- old mentor.
Blossom into that 50-year-old survivor.
Embrace that 60-year-old elder.
Honor that 80-year.-old worshipper
who looks back and smiles.
As she continues to praise God for all He's done.

NEO-Sistah

He called me a Neo-Sistah.
A Newly Empowered Optimistic Sistah.
Driven and determined to win.
Well my head started to spin.
Not from his intoxicating, flattering talk,
but from the confirmation that I am walking the right walk.
See, this Neo-Sistah, used to be a broken vessel.
One who now knows there's a way out of every struggle.
One who once swam in the dark and murky waters of self-hatred.
Disappointment and pain
luxuriated in a sea of self pity and shame.
Hypnotized into believing I could never be enough.
That I am not a combination of the right stuff.
That I could not compare.
This neo-sistah used to live a life of fear.
Scared of the backlash if I dared to dream dreams.
There were many nights fear stifled my screams
and kept my spirit imprisoned in my soul,
but those are now stories of old.
For as I sat in the valley of death
I cried out and asked God to save me.
To break these strongholds and grant me liberty.
No, I'm not speaking religiously,
but I realized my foundation had to be my spirituality.
And faith became the calcium for my bones.
I learned to let praise replace my moans and my groans.
I acknowledged my life was stuck on a replay of auto tunes.
I had to bust out of that cocoon
and show the world the new me.
I also knew I had to share my discovery.
To encourage others to break their chains of mental slavery
this Neo-Sistah had to heal, to forgive, and forget.
And to allow myself to feel
I had to reassure myself that I could love again.
Recalibrate my thinking that all dogs are men

And eliminate my notion that all men are dogs
I had to find a way out of this bitter fog.
And chalk that up to experience.
I had to examine my essence.
To see which of the ingredients attracted the wrong elements to my world.
I uncovered a scared little girl.
One who potentially lives in all of us.
One who struggles to rise from the debris and dust.
To reclaim her queendom.
She fears the loneliness that will come with this new freedom.
She is comfortable hiding within,
but this neo-sistah is driven and determined to win.
So, I nurtured her.
Fed her a daily dose of self-love.
Readied her for the battle.
My pen is my glove.
I prayed hard for her maturity.
For her to open her heart and embrace me;
the neo-sistah I am today.
I am the Queen I am because I pray.
I believe in myself and in every word I say.
Self-awareness anoints my bruised and battered esteem.
I am now inspired to take my dreams
and transform them into my reality.
I know my possibilities are endless.
That each of my steps are God-blessed.
And with Him all things are possible.
He called me a NEO-SISTAH.
A Newly Empowered Optimistic Sistah.
One who is driven and determined to win.
Well my head started to spin.
Not from his intoxicating, flattering talk,
but from the confirmation that I'm walking the right walk.
This Neo-Sistah has found her elixir.
Will you discover yours?

Farewell Endangered One

Why, oh why is it open season on the young, Negro man?
What affliction does he bear that makes him worthless?
How could one just devalue his life for the sake of earthly possessions?
Do they not recognize him as a King of our nation?
In the blink of an eye his life is wiped away?
His importance is ignored.
Who the hell is keeping score of the brothers we've lost?
Of the pain this has caused?
Who cares that somewhere there is a child without a father?
A young wife grieves for her husband.
Who hears the silent cries of a weeping mother as she painfully bids fare well to her only son?
FAREWELL ENDANGERED ONE.
As the sun sets on another day
somewhere in our family another trooper has been taken away.
It is now time to prepare him for his rites of passage.
This is all too familiar.
Did we not do this just yesterday?
Aren't we tired of making the same trip to have our loved sons enter the valley of death?
If this continues, whom will we have left?
How long will this go on?
Look how many are already gone.
Our nation is being wiped out
Our future is becoming a certain doubt.
Stop the killing and realize your worth.
Brothers, you are the fathers of this earth.
Our existence is based on your co-existence with each other.
Please think about that child, that wife and that mother.
As a result of ignorance now they must endure this pain.
Understand the void never to be filled again.
Try to figure out how to pick up the pieces of their life.
Now that their destiny has been changed by a gun or a knife.
Now as hard as it will be

they must go on and all that's left are sweet memories.
Of our ENDANGERED ONE, REST IN PEACE!

Numbers

He gave me an equation so that I could figure out my math.
Me plus He equals success.
Now, I've heard some great advice, but for me that was the best
and it is proven.
I asked him to make me a prime number so that I could only be divided
by me.
And the only ONE who could break me down is He.
To subtract all my weakness
With each decrease, I gained increase.
And my dividends gained interest.
I am blessed.
I asked for a numerical translation.
I got seven.
The math on that number expands mental heavens.
For it took seven days to create the earth and the sea.
And within the first seven He created me.
I am chosen.
I asked to be a power digit even if I stand alone.
Because my purpose comes from theory
and its stamp is on everything I own.
I live life practically
to do God's work spectacularly.
No, I'm not trying to be a hero,
but what are you if you live life as a zero?
I stand to be counted.

From The Cave

I had to retreat to the cave.
When death caused by a recent rave.
Caught the attention of the world
and the murder of a little girl.
Supposedly at her mother's hands.
Mocked the laws of this great land.
I ran for cover.
Marriage is now open to all.
It doesn't matter the sex of your lover.
Freedom and equality for all.
Governing officials continue to fall
and our young kings' pants are still hanging off their ass.
Society is being haunted by ghosts of the past.
I sought shelter because the churches protocol has become so helter-skelter.
I needed to hibernate to see if I, too, could ignore the rise of the black man's death rate,
But it all came to me in a dream.
How AIDS, drugs and domestic violence are eliminating our queens.
This wasn't a dream, this was a nightmare.
Our sons are wearing clothing designed for our daughters to wear.
Our educational system is systematically robbing our children.
There are not enough of us standing up who are qualified to lead them.
Not many worthy enough to say "follow me".
Most who have made up have up and left the community.
Our 40 acres of opportunity are now barren and bare.
Our elders refuse to share wisdom out of fear
of the drug dealers, pimps and hoes.
When will this all stop? Nobody knows.
So, I retreated to the cave.
Not to hide like the rest, but instead to find a way out of this maze
and gain strength as I ready for the battle.
Our future generations are being lead like cattle to the slaughter.
I need help from the village to save our sons and daughters.
The sword God gave me is my pen.
Who will take up their armor and help me?
Save them. Save them. SAVE THEM!

Lost

I'm living in Gotham City.
Looking for Batman.
But all I've found are Jokers.
Searching for a King,
but they're outnumbered by court jesters.
I'm lost because I know you're out there.
I know my pot of bronze molded by God,
and missing a rib that was given to me, is standing in wait.
To shower me in love and bring me security.
Securing me my place as his Queen.
I know, 'cause it's been written.
For in Genesis 2:24 the order was given.
Man must leave his mother and father
and find a Queen with whom he bonds.
When we reach that stage is when we become one.
I know you're out there so I'm not giving up my search.
You come to me in my dreams at night.
We go on long walks and have long talks.
I've seen us playing with our children.
We instill the teachings of our forefathers in their upbringing.
I know you are out there for me
You've inspired my poetry
I've shared my desires with you
Whispered them in your ear
Just before you fade away
And I wake up to my reality
That I'm, living in Gotham City
Looking for Batman,
But all I've found are jokers
Searching for a king,
But they're outnumbered by court jesters
I'm lost because I know you're out there
and I love you.

You

You, you got me twisted.
The way you tease my mind
Causing secretions from my cerebellum
Creating leakage of some of my strongest emotions.
I adore your conversation.
You enlighten me.
You, you release energy.
Energy that has been locked in the minds of pure Nubian royalty
and passed on from generation to generation.
I acknowledge your origination.
Born of the tribes of Abraham.
A lineage educated men still examine.
You've inherited the blessings of a great clan.
I honor your dedication.
Your appreciation for the motherland.
Your respect and edification of a Queen.
Your loyalty and dedication to the ones you glean.
You are King David by design.
Wisdom and strength runs through your bloodline.
I am excited by your potential.
Your keen and certain sense for what is essential.
You epitomize the original African tree.
Your roots are deep and your branches sway in the winds of liberty.
You are the role model our youth need to see.
You, you emulate divinity and your actions identify your sensitivity.
I desire to be your Eve.
To walk beside you.
To lay in the garden and give my Eden to you.
To have you beat my anatomical drums into submission
and cause joy juice to rain down.
I want to recite scriptures with you.
Read from books of ancient times and find examples of you.
I want to celebrate you .

They say that a good black man is a thing of old,
but I've searched and I've found my ancestors resting in your soul.
You, you compose me.
You've been the missing component in my poetry,
and now that you are here I intend to never let my pen run dry.
Because you, you are the answer to my, 'why?'

The Sequel

I still sit back and reminisce on the first time that we made love,
but now instead of a journey we've embarked on a worldwide tour.
You've got me tripping.
Got words of erotica slipping
and joy juice dripping
From my lips
The ancient drums of Africa echoing from my hips.
As I gyrate them, West Indian style
Your tongue takes a lazy walk across my body
And gets buried for a while.
You've mastered the art of seduction
Tested the resilience of my suction.
Expanded my universe
And now I fear, I am cursed.
Plagued by the fire of desire
That you have ignited in my soul.
Damned by a sense of urgency
I need to feel you fill that hole.
The void I sense when I'm not with you I'm channeling.
You make me feel like Jill and Badu under one head wrap.
A poem deserving of an ovation and some finger snaps.
You are my Henry Tanner and I am your collage.
You got me feeling like Nikki and Maya caught up in a ménage
No disrespect to the Queens,
but I'm sure they know what I mean when I say, "You, are creative."
If these were the days of Eros
You, too, would be a famous Greek native.
Like Bussa and Toussaint you have incite a revolution.
Like Martin and Malcolm you know freedom is my only solution.
You make me feel like Dorothy Dandridge.
She, the dancing daughter of Voodoo Priestess of New Orleans.
Me, the poetic daughter of an authentic Barbadian Queen.
Combined, that might cause damage, but you are the master of control.
Your touch indicates that you've studied the techniques of old school lovers.

You've got the passion of Luther and the Levert brothers.
So, baby, hold on to me as we take this journey
and turn it into a worldwide tour.

Your Kinda Love

Being loved by you is an honor.
An honor bestowed upon me.
And I don't know why,
but I am not complaining.
Because your love, that's no ordinary type of love.
You give that floating on a cloud, dancing in the rain,
playing in the autumn leaves kinda love.
The kinda love that reminds me of horses playing in the meadows.
The sounds of their hoofs echoing the beats of our hearts.
The kinda love that takes me on journeys
to exotic places that takes me to peaks.
Higher than the highest mountain and
 brings me back into orbit riding on clouds.
A hot sauce on my chicken.
Collard greens melting in my mouth.
Beef ribs with your special sauce on a hot barbecue grill.
Candied yams saturated in their own sweet,
sticky, brown, juice kinda love.
That nasty, sexy, makes me wanna
scream because I got a piece, kinda love.
A tongue tying, knees knocking, charlie horse cramping kinda love.
That makes me pull my own hair, and slap myself on the ass,
Call out your name, the Creator's, and mine kinda love.
The kinda love that clutters my thoughts and causes my mind to
send off S.O.S. signals over my brain waves.
Announcing that I am consumed.
Consumed by that spiritual, I believe I can fly,
 hallelujah shouting, foot stomping, heal the world, spirit filled kinda love.
When you lay that loving down I am so entranced that my size 16 temple
contorts into positions that only a size 6 should
be able to or so society says.
But with your love all things are possible
and you've shown me how easy it is to love, and be loved.

And it's because of your love
that I'll wake up to the city's early morning calm
and smile as you roll over to kiss me hello.

Distinguish

My government name is Henry Bernard Leslie Gray, but I'd prefer my Hebrew name Melech Meir. I am 21 years of age and I am a writer, poet, singer, rapper, actor, filmmaker, and all around thespian. My stage name is Distinguish and I enjoy performing and learning about new things through performing. All praises due.

Trust

Love used to be number one on my list.
Love used to be something I could never resist.
Now, I'm looking at love like 'you piece of shit'.
Love is blind; no wonder why I couldn't see through her shit.

And her lies before, and her before her.
The her before those, that was only with me for I suppose.
The dough that came along, the checks were pretty long.
The sex ain't never come; no more bread, and then she gone.

Most women I know change to the same sex
'Cause the opposite sex didn't treat them right, or maybe you let
Another person get to know you too fast. What you do instead
Is test the waters, either way, warm or cold, you will get wet.

Some of us giving our time to others, but they still owe.
Some of us giving love to others, but they don't show.
Some of us giving life to others, but they don't grow.
Some of us giving seeds to others, but they don't sow.

Most relationships out here are lacking trust.
If I don't trust myself how can I trust you well enough.
If myself comes first, but I'm not well enough.
So, now the pressures on you. Well, have you had enough?

Don't talk about sex and giving head if you don't love yourself.
'Cause filling a void from what you think your life is missing
is weakening your health.
If you're a female and think the majority of men holla too much
don't respond, but that doesn't mean you shouldn't want to smile or
blush.

And fellas, every girl is not a pop.
She may give you the eye, but that girl ain't a chicken
 and she is not a "Popeye's".
Teenagers nowadays don't value sex as much as they did.
So, I'm not surprised if a new teenage mother already got 3 kids.

If God blesses me with a child then I'm naming it Trust.
It will not suffer for my sins that I've helped to grow up.
I love women with a passion,
But don't mean I have to seatbelt and fasten.
Just because my mind is already on smashing.

~To love me, I must be able to TRUST you, and you must able to TRUST me.

Analytical

A huge canvas is filled.
Thoughts are never really harnessed.
Lies hurt every infrastructure of the muscle.
The truth hurts, doesn't it?

Can you look at what you're looking at while the looked at object is being looked at?
Pain is hard to fathom and to put in words when words are nothing, but words.
Questions start to arise like: What is life like? What's what without something right?
Too deep to look into brains missing a few screws thinking about last night who screwed.

Lens need to be redefined because people have defined it from a book that came from books.
Skin deep beauty needs a face-lift the surface needs a virtuous tone of adjustment.
Things aren't just things, a word made up to justify the means.
We put things in between, but not saying a thing.

Let us make let us in our image.
Imagine making us letting.
Or us letting making our in image
The bible is written too confusingly as well.

Boy Positive

Hi, my name is Vic and I've dated some of the baddest girls around. Some of them gave me things that you guys wouldn't want. Not because of baggage or anything like that, but because you wouldn't want to keep it. Being a playa wasn't the easiest thing. Pimpin ain't, easy you know. You better take notes, but nah, anything I say about my current girl-friend tonight then remember this: Love kills more than *DWIs* and *DW-HIGHS*.

Her name was Mydia.
And every chance I had to myself I tried to get rid of her.
Past relationships, her partners weren't seeking testing 'cause peoples symptoms were silent.
And every time I told her I think you got a problem she turned more violent.
We lasted for about 2 weeks due to heavy exposure.
Then I spoke to celibacy 'cause keeping it a buck made me wanna save a buck after I told Duane Reade to keep their condoms.
I probably should've hollered at abstinence when we first started, but slowly I was bombarded by her sister Nor Rhea'.
See, Nor Rhea was my ex, but she, well, I knew the real her before we even thought about sex.
I should've known that having a threesome would've been a health consequence.
So, I've been seeking treatment ever since.
Treatment told me to holla at antibiotics and I was like that's it for the both of them.
Treatment said, "Yeah, so I broke off the affair without a worry, doubt and a care.
Rhea gave one of my mans PID and I cried at his wake, but he ain't never wake. Messing with that type of girl was a huge mistake.
Ya'll wanna hear something crazy, last night this girl HPV called me and said she had a crush on me, but she's asymptomatic so you know I ain't even know.
But on average she tells 6.2 million other guys that same story.
I knew she was trouble, but I took her down anyway.

It's like 100 types of that girl, but 30 of them are sexually transmitted, she said "Vic, you fitted the description."
Man, I thought she was trippin', so I called up my mistress Phyllis and we got straight to the dippin'.
And everything was cool cause we would skip school and blow a whole weekend to get those extra sexual healings in our systems.
But then she hit me with the news.
Talking 'bout she had a rash. I thought it was a joke so I laughed, but then she lifted up her shirt and showed me her lesions.
Told me her nickname was the great imitator. Going on about how she causes unintentional ulcers that seem painless, but if untreated symptoms develop 10 to 20 years after infection that lead to numbness, blindness, and even death; next!
See, I dated all of these girls not realizing it was one playing me this whole time. She shape-shifted and gave herpes kisses that made diseases that causes me to be at dis-ease and I pissed blood. My red and white t-cells celebrated Christmas inside of me. I was the tree, I was the big T. Rhea was actually Gonorrhea, Mydia was really Chlamydia and Phyllis was really Syphilis.
Their ornaments lay dormant on my branches causing rashes, lesions and kidney failure. MY CD4 cells suffered, oh what I wouldn't give to see C4 bombs explode.
We exchanged bodily fluids for bodily organs. I gave her my heart and she gave it a heart that takes shape of what's important. What I thought was sort of love gave me HIV. Now I can't get rid of her, it's never over. I told you in the beginning of this poem that my name was Vic. Well, it's short for victim.
The ends never justify the means because in the end it's always mean. Well, at least for me. Aside from this poem, these pills I take won't stop HIV from growing inside of me.

If I Was A Poet

If I was a poet I'd throw my poem off all-altering acoustic acid allergy acne alliteration and watch it stop conversations like your head upside down stopping blood circulation and make it do a back flip. Pilf kcab. Saying words backwards into the air like gymnastics.
If I was a poet I'd acrobat acronyms from gospel hymns that sing so you could get the message. I'd turn my poem into a song so it can even be sung from a broken record.
If I was a poet I'd turn back the hands of time and stop Eve from eating the forbidden fruit and give Adam back mankind.
If I was a poet I'd pull off enough touts and push out eternal thoughts until Gods God-self put God on the cross. If I was a poet I'd crack more skulls than cracked whips on the backs of slaves and show you what a headache is. Slave masters can't whip cracks like community pharmacist on the strip 'cause prostitutes too slow 'cause John loves tricks.
If I was a poet I'd watch you listen to my poem as it turns you on. Getting you all aroused like you're by yourself in a room. Thoughts are stimulated faster than a test drive simulation or immigrants assimilated in the United States of Atheist.
If I was a poet I'd sing a song from Solomon and tell him how dark the shade is. And watch Satan conduct the musical called,"The World's Rapist". And see God put the whole thing on Discovery Kids 'cause the History Channel is too busy talking about myths.
If I was a poet, I'd set Asar Anpu
Be in tune black as the universe I'm so Heru.
 If I was a poet, I'd Medgar Evers Amiri Baracka Roy Wilkins till X's covered the white house building and Dr. King our children, but tell'em to stop dreaming 'cause Nat Turner is in the back ground talking to Huey P. about Newton more shots at empty dark holes than semen 'cause Che Guevara is screaming "La Revolution" while Patrice Lumumba is taking a beating.
Tupac is sighing because his own people won't come to his defense. Billie Holidays strange fruit still has a bite mark from that garden as August Wilson takes down his fences.

If I was a poet, I'd take my glasses off and allow you to see through my lenses and we'd all share the same senses and boycott the census and serve the same life sentence.
If I Was A Poet.

Her Stories Through History

I say those little girls need their freedom.
Those little girls need their freedom.
Those little girls need their freedom.
Those little girls need their freedom.
Her story got bombarded.
Most teens growing up don't know who Rosa Parks is.
Harriet's Tub got men by the facet,
and Billie needs a holiday that tree bears chocolate.
Things ain't strange anymore, but we got more fruit.
Trees grow, but they still come from bad roots.
Helena Lacks cells still breed hepatitis.
Modern day Moses touch the bush and catch the AIDS virus.
So, when they die they won't rise in 3 days.
They're lazy. Still, this Lazarus here wants his pay.
Angela Davis might send a panther his way
or call Assata for the OK on an AK.
Not to spray, but to build black truce.
Word to Coretta Scott King and Sojourner Truth.
Anita's nowadays ain't baking hit records, some say.
It's more like the player's club and she's a diamond in every way.
Madame C.J. Walker, women thank you for their hair products.
Even though their smoking scalps off harder than narcotics .
We don't have any more Mary Jane Watsons
or anymore modern day Betty Stocktons.
Our nowadays Hattie McDaniels are gone with the wind.
What happened to dreams like May Jemison?
We will never forget Latisha Harlin, but
that riot in L.A. didn't solve any problems.
It is no mystery that his stories
would be nothing without her stories.

The Ankh

I carry the ankh.
If Horus hadn't been hated by his brother
the symbolism of his phallus wouldn't be beneficial to his lover.
This is for my brothers that mourn. All my brothers come on.
We ain't gonna read the poem, learn a little, and verse one.
The Ankh, known as the key of life,
key of the Nile, or Crux Ansata. Please say it right.
Egyptian gods carried it by the loop in the middle.
This key opened up doors, big or small; enormous or little.
The Ankh appears frequently in Egyptian tomb paintings.
That cross you wear came from the Ankh. Don't get it sadly mistaken.
My Ba gives off a lot of Akh still feeding this knowledge Ka.
Heru, the falcon or the hawk—y'all really don't want me to start.
Hieroglyphic filtered Egyptian walls. You've taken what does not belong
to you, or the letter "U". Hmph, you look just like you.
Whoever calls the Ankh pagan doesn't know his-story or her-story.
What books are you reading? Oh, those filled with allegories.
Adam and Eve's story came from Osiris and Isis and Heru's story was
fabricated to give you what Christ is.
We misplaced our spirituality for the world's vanity and no longer want
to know thyself.
So, instead of reading books for this knowledge we never
go back to school to be scholars.
The Ankh should be a symbol for those who see it understand the
universe and thyself as someone Sirius.
The ancient people of Kemet knew themselves as the royal lineage.
So, any thoughts you had that differs from what I've stated should end
now like periods.
What happens when you fold a belt, when you fold a whip, Ankh's across
the chest?
Your pants loop all out there in the open like exposure is.
The Egyptian way of life dealt with peace and prosperity
while history books display war, blood and vulgar authority.
The ankh also symbolizes harmony between the man and the woman.

But what happened? The world painted the picture that she's no longer good looking.
I carry the ANKH.

We Are The Liars Of The Truth

Cringe, bite the lip, skin the teeth and moan in agony that the naked eye can fathom so the visible will be closed shut. Reach, scream at the top of your lungs 'til the air can no longer suck in and allow the wind to be suffocated in the atmosphere. Beg for the, not too seen, distant future and allow the past to be forgiven as much as you don't want it to. What is not unforgivable? Even Christ gave his life for the sins of sinners who disobey constantly and repent as a lie and then the life is not deceived. Wrong. People deceive it. Receive it in different amounts of ways. The ultimate change is just to change.

Accept the inevitable truth as it comes, and bites the tongue that has life and death as a dictatorship. Because when you're the only one who cares about the lie the truth then becomes it eventually. And people stop caring about the truth because they've lied so much to make it true. Nobody forgets the truth you just become better liars!

And so, alas, the dingy despicable spec of particles that hurt each gland in the anatomy has now found some way to make it's physical shell acceptable to the worlds surface as the sun pours yellow surprise into the stony skull that has now acquired hate, anguish, and stubbornness over the years.

Hard brick pain. It hurts. Yell. Scream. Cry. Hate everything you have ever known and compromise your emotions. Go against your will to feel. Go against your heart to love. Go against your thoughts to think. Go against the grain as you take 39 lashes, but you have never taken 39 lashes like he did. We are the liars of the truth. If we cannot accept the truths and lies that we so often tell, then how can we forgive the truth of a lie and the lie of a truth that we tell?

The Black Woman's Standards

Maybe if you'd wear less provocative clothing
Men's mouths would be shut. So, nothing they think, stupid, is spoken.
An insult wouldn't be an insult, but more like a joking.
A short skirt or an unbuttoned blouse would read, "Stop Hoping".
What if a female had the power to read a man's mind
before she'd let him inside her gate and black behind?
What if a woman could stop a man from thinking about sex as an object
and more like a privilege?
So, babies that are being born would seem harmless.
Maury is making millions off paternity tests.
Women aren't you stressed to go to another man to find the father of
your child is properly fed?
Man it's a game how we seek to get attention 'cause it's based on how
we dress.
Love is lust, and sex might as well be due to the resistance of the flesh.
Your behind is peeking out—every other head turns.
The avenue in the hood wants its own turn.
Every day you do this like you love to stunt.
Think about it, you've convinced yourself that you're nothing without
your chest and butt.
Daddy's little girls are running the block.
Tell Idris Elba he gonna need more than hot grits and pots.
All women are the ones who can change their standards.
Our men have lost their belts so they're in need of some hangers.
No manners. Why she gotta be a B----?
Does she have four legs, does she bark, does she piss all out in public
without flushing her waste?
I just painted that picture. You probably don't like the taste.
Women, you should make getting the goodies harder.
Then you wouldn't be wrong on who is and who is not the father.
You wouldn't look ridiculous on TV; Jerry Springer and Maury.
Be like a battlefield: Pride & Glory.
But I know there are some who will look at this
and shake their heads (I know you'll shake it chick).

Go to a party and meet a "nice guy"
and use protection.
Wait a minute don't lie!
Ok, some will and some won't.
Any disease though is no joke and I quote:
"Men lie, women lie; numbers don't."
Check the statistics 'cause AIDS is killing off most black folks.
Black teenagers, black women.
Even if contraception were used in the beginning
your body is a temple so treat it as such.
But your body is **your body.**
I'm just a poet it's not like I know much; right.
You've lost that standard.
Now, I can approach you with my pants half off my waist.
A Yankee fitted on and a beat up screwed face.
Sneakers on my feet—untied shoe lace.
Your behind caught my eyes, you ain't all that fine, but I can't tell you
that I have to have intercourse.
Condoms were made to last 3 minutes so if it pops, you're a pop,
anyways I'll go raw, ah honey take a chance, girl I'm clean.
When was the last time you were tested for HIV?
Were you ever put at risk?
Do you have multiple partners?
Do you love to kiss?
If you're standards were set high there'd be no need to ask you this.
If you're standards are set high teach it to the kids!
Especially those who are promiscuous or seem to be sexually active.
Sex was never a problem you've just abused you're gift.
Women who give it up early and easy remind me of stepping in…
It's easy to get into and hard to get out of.
So please women redefine your standards.
Melech Meir, one love.

Womentors

Asa lead the victims to safety,
suffering from slavery;
Brothers and sisters lead the way.
Mr. Cheatham on the podium speaking,
Liberation versus freedom, those like minded
 Versus those most likely to wind up bleeding.
Ms. Danields talking about sharing the light and love
with everybody in the universe because they should love.
We all have a power tool, without 40 acres and a mule,
Still spiking, doing the right thing still in a daze, school.
Honest Abe gives me constructive criticism on my writing,
While intellect heightens.
Those younger are now enlightened.
E just sent a message to congress about us fighting,
but what's civil in our lives if we can't live too exciting?
You can always count on Deep Man having his sword in his clutch,
When he speaks, the world is silent but if you are not now; hush.
Jeho Hanan always broke bread with me in August Martin and told me
This is going to be a lonely road when I was starting. He also said I need
to build my followers, more disciples,
but I don't necessarily think he meant by the bible.
Harold Mathieu, who I just met, helped me sought out my feelings and
what he means to me already has a deeper meaning.
Robert Turner, who I admired from the first day I met him, he taught me
dancing is a way of life so I love sweating.
Victoria Bond, who teaches me English at John Jay, got me seeking more
distance. Pushing myself in ways that I never knew I could push. I'd give
pregnant women a run for their babies when giving birth to them.
Thank you for the here moments, right now. I'll be keeping them!
Mommy and Daddy, words go without saying. You're the reason I am a
reason and this great reason for saying. My mentors who are young and
old inspire me.
Love your mentors.
P.S. I need to step up my womentors!

Food For Thought

I could have more than one—David had a few.
I'm only just a man. This is what some men like to do.
Not by force, mostly by attraction.
This just isn't a poem. I'm not just only rapping.
In many different cultures, they like to have choices.
The mothers of all living things, we help them to find their voices.
Who are we? Is that what you are asking?
The sons from the Adam, ask Sosa and Michael Jackson.
What you consider cheating, we consider multiplication.
What you know as a test we know as a demonstration.
You condemn what you fear, and we fear what you condemn.
That's we can't tell the boys from the girls,
you took the Wo from the Men!
Incest all across the land, temptation's hard to resist.
Most of us yield to our lust then catch herpes or syphilis.
Due to an involuntary kiss, why are we so promiscuous?
So quick to lick any breast, so quick to suck any...
We're idiots, that's right, we are all victims
Sin today, pray tomorrow, next week from now we're back to that...
No wonder why we're all born between urine and feces.
Some of us eat from it today and we wonder why diseases increases.
Just because she loves you don't mean she's the cleanest.
Just because he hugs you don't mean he'll wash your dishes.
We talk so expensive, but end up the cheapest.
You wouldn't get far, but how do you not acknowledge Jesus?
Stuck in denial like Peter, a traitor like Judas.
You *follow* like Muhammad and bald heads like Buddhas.
Put *"life"* in a statue, and praise made up rulers
Our kids have been lied to; they're not the future!

All Flowin' Big Mama

All Flowin', born Antoinette Davis, created a forum for poets to create and give back to the community. Coming from a troubled past and she uses her talents, a gift from God, to heal, inspire and uplift.

All Flowin' is the founder of Creative Minds Poetry Club of Mercy College. Through the club she has helped other poets find their stage presence as well as a community heart as they raise money for worthy causes through poetry. She is also the one of the co-founders of Urban Trilogy, a small group dedicated to making changes through poetry.

All Flowin' was instrumental in raising funds and awareness for causes such as hurricane Katrina, domestic violence, AIDS and Feed the Children. She believes everyone has a poetic voice and because of this developed "Lead the Future" for college poets to mentor at public schools.

All Flowin' is blessed with two talented children who have graced her existence. She works full-time with the Administration for Child Services, and is currently pursuing a Masters Degree in Family Counseling.

Trying to bring awareness through her words her motto is, "There is laughter and learning seen through everything". Her sentiment, "If only one person reads my words believe me I have touched many."

Through these eyes

Through these eyes I allow you to travel through time.
Allow your mind to grace the pages of our history.
Through these eyes I allow you to feel the swelling of my loins and the expansion of my womb.
As I create, cultivate, and generate life though these eyes my sweat and tears borne the existences of culture.
It's through my eyes you will see the pain and sacrifices endured to birth nations, countries and civilizations.
See, my eyes are narrow described to be feline natured to carry the tales no other holds.
It is the cotton picked from the plantation of my soul that brought the fruit of generations hung by others.
But through these eyes I have created the pickers as well as the hangers
It is through these eyes that I bare the injustices on my spirit and give you the insight to brave on.
My eyes have seen the creation and destruction of worlds.
I have stood tall and reared the best and the worst.
I have stood alone to rebuild and reconstruct devastation.
My eyes have enticed leaders, encourage reform and move mountains.
Stare through these eyes to see your conception.
The manifestation of your power that first pulsated through my veins giving you the identity you now hold.
It's through these eyes my eyes, the eyes of a woman
that the truth of history can be learned and shared.

Smarter Than a Fifth Grader

I don't wanna grow up and I am not a Toy R Us kid.
My ambitions are higher than most children give.
My ideals and dreams are straighter.
My goal is to be smarter than the average fifth grader.
I want to remember facts embedded in my brain.
Information I thought I'd never use again.
Like one plus two minus X divided six cubed
Equals a sum equivalent to, but not greater than one
Or something like that to prove I'm not dumb.
I want to know the distance between two trains
If one left New York at two and the other left Baltimore at three.
What would the calculated speed be and in which direction it goes?
And in the long run how does it affect me?
These are the average facts a fifth grader knows?
I want to know the highest point of the highest mountain.
Did Ponce de Leon find his magic fountain?
What era did crusades begins and how did world wars end?
I wanna list every president who ran this country
In order of their entry.
I wanna get my facts and information in line.
So, when I step to the podium for the first time
the announcer can announce with pride.
Here is the first college student who is actually smarter
than the average fifth grader.

For H.I.M. Verbal Waters

I approached him nearly void of life.
Dehydrated and gasping for more.
Turned off by the mishaps of past adventures.
Internally bruised and seeking hope
I allow myself to fall into his arms.
Gathered in his embrace he sprinkled my face with his verbal waters.
Rejuvenating my essence and rebuilding my soul.
I allowed him to bathe me in verbal waters.
Healing my pains and bandaging my past wounds.
He replaced the blood in my veins with words,
ideals, and hope allowing me to spit knowledge.
Reconstruct the shambles of hope that once dwelled in my heart.
Giving love a womb to grow and develop
I open my mouth, as I taste his intellect on my lips
allowing my mental to open a new brave of communication.
And have my fears and inhibitions drain from my body.
As I allow him to wash me from head to toe with his verbal waters.

Extend Your Hand Across the Sea

Extend your hand across the sea
To repair broken souls and shattered hearts
To rebuild dreams that can crumble to the earth
As the world moved beneath their feet
Help relieve the hunger that grows
Extend your hand to help answer the cries still heard
As families are forever broken and ties forever cut
As house is no longer homes and children are left to fend alone
As the things we take for granted are as precious as gold
Extend a hand to wipe the tears that will forever fall
As the cries rise to the heaven to greet those who were lost
As children fall to their knee in desperation and need
As mothers morn children who will never live a dream

Extend a hand to share the compassion beating within your chest
Release the emotion that holds eyes to the sight of destruction
That makes you stop breathing as scenes flash across the screen
React to the desire to extend a hand.

Confidence

I transcend oceans
Moving through time and space
Never allowing color to guide me
Never allowing races to hinder me
I carry many meanings
Holding value for all
I portray love
And deliver hate
I depict innocence
And describe guilt
I am the essence of language
Without me there is silence
I am confident in my existence
Knowing without me there is nothing
Knowing I hold the keys to many doors
Doors leading to the past, future, and present
I carry tales of lessons learned and forgotten
I can hold my own 'cause I am needed by all
I am the essential of life
I am the epitome of communication
I am...words.

Heartbeat of the City

Do you hear it?
Bom, bom, bom, bom.
From beneath my feet I hear the internal sound of the city's heartbeat
The constant ticking that gives the city life
The rhythm that never flat lines
Allowing souls of the past to inherit new ones
Passing stories and talent from generation to generation
Hearing excuse me, excuse me, may I get your attention?
From the essences of one's spirit
As it is possessed by heat beat of the city.
I am here to entertain you, to allow you to relive history as I stand in this train car and bare myself in hopes you smile as my past stood on these platforms with the same hopes and dreams many years before me.
I ask you, do you hear the bom bom bom bom?
Under your feet the sound of tradition and culture that won't sleep
The rhythm of words, songs and dance wrap tight in music
The heart of the city lies beneath your feet
if you will only be still for a moment you can hear it.
Bom bom bom please stand clear of the closing doors

Defined

Who are you?
Are you the soul that shares my essence?
Are you the spirit who shares my space?
Are you the one promise from God?
The one foreseen in my dreams
The one who completes my means.

Who are you?
Are you the one who starts my heart?
The one who makes my whole being jump
The one who leaves no secret unlocked
The one who brings out the sun
The one to whom my true self belongs

Not knowing who you are let me tell you who I am
I am the reason the moon shines so bright
The reason lovers give long kisses goodnight
The reason the sun goes down at night
I am the last piece of the puzzle that leads to completion
I am the missing link to all life's mysteries

Who am I?
I am the feeling you get when you win
I am the first puff to a smoker
I am the first drink to a drinker
I am the first bite to a taster
I am the intoxication of all life's pleasures

Who are we?
We are the destiny of the future
We are the hope of freewill
We are the spectrum of light that will travel on forever
We are formulations of education that was meant to teach the masses

We are the determination of all repressed nations
We are the voice in the sea of quiet
We are the innovations of all life equations

Who are you?
Who am I?
Who are we?
We are together separate
We are apart together
We are designs formed in the sand
We are waves of the tide that carries the sand away
Together we are defined
Separate we are unknown
who are we does anyone really know!

Innocence's Prayer

Star light star bright first star I see tonight
I wish I may I wish I might have this prayer
I pray tonight

As I stare into the sky I pray that hunger I feel will go away
I pray the night will come quickly to hide my fear of starving another day
I pray that my words are food
And thoughts are nutrients
That every time I speak or think
My mind and body will grow strong

I feel my prayers fall on deaf ears
As I watch my family grows in amount but diminish in size
As watch my friends eyes sink in and belly grow big
Because of lack of sustenance
As I struggle to survive
And pray that help will soon arrive

Star light star bright any star I see tonight
I wish I may I wish I might have this dream
I dream to night

As I lay in my bed and close my eyes
I prepare myself sleep in hope of dreaming
I dream that food is as abundant as air
I dream that land is fertile
And like a tree I grow

I pray That there is enough money to share
And crop fields aren't bare
I dream and pray to grow strong and tall
In hopes to help famine disappear

As the sky fills with clouds
I rise from bended knee
And hope the bright star heard me
Because when all is said and done
And I wake to the morning sun
I am still hungry

Broken Chains

I've waded in my share of waters
And climbed the wrong side of many mountains
To conquer my past and secure my future
See I am the slave woman's dream
And the slave master's fear
I am the branches embedded in my ancestors back
And each goal accomplished I uproot the trees from their skins
Leaving them bare and beautiful
I am the limbs that swung low
With bodies of my heritage
Hung by ropes to end prayers
But I pray on
As I march on
March through my history
Changing my past to correct my future
Stepping in the footsteps of my leaders
Riding the rail of the underground
To discover the freedom of my mind
Let loose the knowledge held captive
By decades of injustices
I don't swing by vines
Like the savages, I'm portrayed to be
Be sling word of intelligence
Like the person I was meant to be
My hands were not designed to destroy
But were formulated to create
I was born with innate desire
To stand tall away from the auction block
To gather my friends and keep my family
To cherish unity
Alone I am single, but with a single dream
Hush I hear someone calling my name
And it's through the rivers of tears
Cried by a slave I swam
Carrying hope on one shoulder and strength on the other

Strength to endure another day
Strength to leave my broken chains on the side of the road
No longer using the weight of my past to hold me back
I am my past, but through it I become a better future
With every barrier I break
I prove history is a lesson learned
Not to be repeated or forgot

Untold

I want to open my soul to you
Have you read me like a book
Have you turn the pages of my history
And grasp a better look
Want you to use your fingertips
And read my body like Braille
I want to share my spirit with you
And have you travel through my mind
Have you stare into my eyes
And stop the movement of time
Engulf you into my body
Without actual touch
Oh I want to tell you so much
How the wind kisses my cheek
When I know you're near
How rain dances on my lips
To cover up my fears
How my heart skips two beats
Just with your thoughts
How my dark corners
Now shine bright
I want to say I love you
Without words without sound without touch
I want to show emotions I've hidden so deep
I want to say I love you without showing defeat
I want each tear drop
To tell you a tale
Of my past, of present, of future
Of my pain, of my loss, of my loves
I want to share my soul with you
I want to say I love you
But instead I just say
I care.

ARIES

Michael "Aries" Trowell was born and raised in Brooklyn, New York. His love for spoken word was expressed at a young age. His passion for poetry was born out of his love for Hip Hop. As a citizen of New York City's poetry community, Aries, as he's known on stage, has performed and hosted many shows including Nuyorican Poets Cafe, S.O.B.'s and Groove N.Y.C.

He has also played a very intricate part as one of the three hosts of the internet radio show Three Ingredients, One Foundation on The JayEveryday Radio alongside phenomenal poets, Empress Poetry and K.L. Belvin.

Aries is also a songwriter, music producer, and has worked with many influential R&B soul artists like Dwele, Raheem Devaughn, Javier Colon and others.

Aries is a full-time Educator and uses his God-given talent as a tool to teach mentally and emotionally challenged pre-school students and uses his love of poetry as a bridge to teach children how to read, recognize letters, and rhyming words.

Aries is a loving and devoted Husband, Father and loyal Friend.

1000 Kisses

If I have kissed you once,
I have kissed you 1000 times.
Each morning as I arise.
Each night as I drift to sleep.
Each hour of every day.
Each moment before it goes away.

The kisses shared between you and I,
Have many times reached the sky.
As your lips part and anxiousness increases,
Your heart pounds and breathing ceases.

My lips leap to yours hungry for the taste.
Sweetness drips from you to me.
As desire grows, my heart races.
Inches apart seem as miles waiting.

The miles increase as space shortens.
Time appears to stand still.
So close yet so far.
When? Now, please, now?

Once more, 1001.
Make it 2, so many more.
Caressing ever caressing those
Tender lips, each time as the first.

If I have kissed you 1000 times,
I would give them all away
To make the dream a reality,
And kiss you once.

Apology

How do I tell you I'm sorry?
With a gesture, a look, a touch.
How is it I never realized
I hurt you so very much?

I do not ask forgiveness,
A comfort I'll never deserve.
I merely want to let you know,
But I cannot find the nerve.

To finally confront you, face-to-face,
To look you in the eye,
To face your wrath, your apathy.
Too terrified to try.

You called me a liar. I turned away.
I festered and I fled.
Cutting and wounding and lashing out,
Just to see if you bled.

Betraying and deceiving you,
I surely had no right.
To snatch away such a precious gem;
A dark thief in the night.

Two years and forever passed
To bring us to this day,
When I present these simple words
I never thought to say.

The time has come, it's long past due,
To put aside my fear;
Would this confession torture you,
Or have you longed to hear?

To hear those two forbidden words,
To vanquish all the pain,
To understand my dearest wish
To know you once again.

The years aged me remarkably,
Though they have not made me wise;
I do know I erred irrevocably
For that, I apologize.

I LISTEN

I LISTEN to a song until I understand the artists thoughts, intentions, emotions that rattle behind the notes, melodies, drum hits and bass lines.
I READ a song's lyrics until I truly understand their line of thinking, their reason for writing it, their intentions, their thought process.
I BUY an album when I am truly inspired, more energized to pay money for a recording of songs not tampered by pirated software, but enhanced by a touch of self pride, personal ownership, and human effort.
I PRAISE all artists big and small obsessed with being original, overcome with a sense of purpose, to entertain, to show off, to show progress, to display one's talents, to inspire.
I LISTEN to music that makes me think, that makes me stop dead in my tracks like time just froze. And all I can think about is that guitar riff that shook me all night long or that low note by Chuck Berry that awed me, or that drum solo that had me tappin' my foot to a rhythm I never knew before.
I LISTEN to people who invoke conversation, a smile, laughter, guttural laughter, politics, anger, controversy and a love for the human spirit.
I LISTEN to a song until I understand the artist's thoughts, intentions, emotions that rattle behind the notes, melodies, drum hits and bass lines.

Artistic Inspiration

Is it really real?
Is this love coming from a true source
Or am I filled with a remorse of love
that once was or could have been?
'Cause back when I was worldly and naive to the ways of the heart.
I treated love as if it were art with light colors of trust and understanding
and dark hues of jealousy and anger with contrasts of lust and passion.
I painted my love on uncertain canvases of discovery with light
brushstrokes of moonlight walks
and after midnight talks of nothing unparticular.
Long deep strokes of passion and ecstasy across the palate of your body
As we slip into a trance that Van Gogh's on forever.
In creeps dark violent blotches of mistrust leading to crimson deep
Arguments that run down the canvas as thick as blood easily escalating to
The point of no return.
When emotions ease onto the canvas
Creating a white spread of soft apologies
Seemingly erasing all traces of pain
 that coated the canvas so that love can start anew.
Back and forth, Forth and back this cycle continued until a sigh of relief.
I stepped back to admire my work of art
Only to be met with feelings of confusion.
To the left dark and violent storms of doubt and misunderstanding, to the
right sunny days of confidence and security, and in the middle a heart,
plump, vibrant and filled with love, but the heart was broken.

I Love You

I love you
Because the Earth turns around the sun
Because the North wind blows north sometimes
Because the Pope is Catholic and most Rabbis Jewish
Because winters flow into springs and the air clears after a storm
Because only my love for you despite the charms or gravity keeps me from falling off this Earth into another dimension
I love you because it is the natural order of things
I love you like the habit I picked up in college of sleeping through lectures or saying I'm sorry when I get stopped for speeding.
Because I drink a glass of water in the morning and use Facebook all through the day
Because I take my coffee Black and my milk with chocolate
Because you keep my feet warm, though my life is a mess
I love you because I don't want it any other way
I am helpless in my love for you
It makes me so happy to hear you call my name
I am amazed you can resist locking me in an echo chamber where your voice reverberates through the four walls sending me into spasmodic ecstasy
I love you because it's been so good for so long that if I didn't love you I'd have to be born again and that is not a theological statement
I am pitiful in my love for you
The Dells tell me Love is so simple
The thought though of you sends indescribably delicious thrills throughout and through-in my body
I love you because I am afraid of the dark and can't sleep in the light
Because I rub my eyes when I wake up in the morning and find you there
Because you, with all your magic powers, were determined that I should love you
Because there was nothing for you, but that I would love you
I love you because you made me want to love you more than I love my privacy, my freedom, my commitments, and responsibilities
I love you 'cause I changed my life to love you

Because you saw me one Friday evening at D&B and decided that I would love you
I love you, I love you, I love you.

I'd Die

I'd die for her.
Bold statement for someone who's never truly lived.
Biding all his time on the safe side of life.
Never really living out any of his true dreams.
Not realizing this reality isn't really what it seems.
Focusing on the exterior, ignoring the interior,
he wears his life on his back.
Not worrying about dreams or aspirations.
Only concerned with fact.
What is tangible or within his grasp,
Only enough time to make it.
But not enough to make it last.
"Live for today" is his motto.
"You're not promised tomorrow"
Moving at the speed of life no time for happiness
Or sorrow or regret or despair or love
Forgetting the essentials of what it means to, actually, live.

Love Is An Emotion

Love is an emotion. The ultimate emotion where all words are mixed into one and it does it with such devotion.

When I got involved with love my head spun, 'cause when I got with the girl I thought was the one and did everything for her that was allowed under the sun not knowing she was toying with my heart for fun as she chewed up my soul and spit it out like gum.

Damn, that love is like a wild horse and if you fall off you know what they say. "You gotta get back up there and ride", but what about how you feel inside? When your life is on a down slide and all you wanna do is hide, but what's keeping you going is your pride. It's telling you not to give in, you've been through worse ruin, but little do you know, you're setting yourself up for it to happen again!

But don't get me wrong, there is a rare love. A love that's sent from the heaven above where even a petty argument is unheard of. Where there are flowers and candy given on Valentine's day & phone calls made in the middle of the night just to say I Love You!

That's where I wanna be, or is loneliness my destiny? I just want someone to love me for me so I can love them for eternity 'cause, right now, emptiness is my reality and this love S**T is just a fallacy!

Marriage

You finally found each other after searching hard for love.
In this uncertain world you've come to one you're certain of.
How can you know the someone whom you'll cherish throughout life?
What identifies a husband or a wife?
Sometimes there's a gravity.
Sudden, fierce, obsessed.
As if you're falling towards some star,
By its strong pull possessed.
Or sometimes there's a childhood sense
Of unselfconscious grace
Sustained within the safety zone
Of unprovoked embrace.
Sometimes there's the terror of
The searing pain of grief.
As if the loss of love were death:
Sheer scream without relief.
Or there's a sense of loveliness.
Too precious to be lost.
A gift of all that makes life good,
Beyond constraint or cost.
Whatever signs you read, they all
Point in the same direction.
The self that lies beyond the self
In love and shared affection.
True love lies far beyond the will,
Yet you must choose to love.
Each day to put aside the self
And with the angels move.

Nigger

I was born just like my Great Grandfather, a Nigger.
A hundred years ago, but my future paints the same picture.
Will my sons travel the same roads that ole' pops laid
or will the rain wash away those tracks and stop pain?
Can the sun shine that bright, so everyone is blind?
No more seeing black or white, if everyone could find.
The real meaning of love, happiness and truth sublime.
These are the words of all niggers, dead and left behind.
Even the ones that submitted to racism in their own minds.
The hate they endured, it's no wonder they stop trying.
I love the nigger lady in front of the bus because she declined.
I love the nigger man that told all of us we couldn't eat swine.
I love the nigger that made niggers and non niggers march as one.
I love the nigger that gave triggers and armed niggers to guard the slums.
I love all niggers, enslaved daughters and sons, and even the free ones.
Niggers martyred and hung, niggers scarred and shunned, niggers
swallowed their tongues, and I love the last nigger, at last, you will come.

Rain

Assume the shape of water
spread out on the table and stay a while.
Seeping into every pore of my skin.
Escape to the sky hiding behind thunder,
sharing a secret with lightning.
Pound mountains to dust and carry them on your back,
handful by handful.
Find me lost in you wishing to taste the
scent of you as you rock me to sleep.

Reality

Reality is that slap in the face.
When you think you have the world by the tail
and life seems to be moving at your own pace.
When you feel like there is no way you can fail.
Reality is there to open your eyes.
When you find you were walking with them closed
And it shows you a sight that can surely make you cry.
Because with reality, it shows you what you already know.
Reality breaks a person's heart and soul
And destroys dreams and hopes that a person feels.
The truth and only truth is reality's only goal.
And it doesn't care whose world that it might kill.
Reality keeps me in a state of mind
That I know it has complete control.
But sometimes my dreams overtake reality I find
And love lives for a while in my heart and soul.
Reality is not fair.
Reality does not care.

K`larity

KiKi "K`larity" Johnson hails from New York City and currently resides in the Hampton Roads area of Virginia. She attended Norfolk State University and majored in Psychology with a focus on Elementary Education.

Her optimistic ability to shed "clarity" and wisdom on life's adversities helped a very close friend to derive her pen-name. K`larity has been writing and sharing poetry since the age of fourteen and her work has been featured in several online and print publications, including: Poetica Magazine; Urban Tymes. K`larity also placed as a runner up for an HBO poetry contest.

While still in high school one of her first creative writing essays and original poems was recognized, translated in Italian and published in an international foreign language journal.

Frequently, K`larity shares her written works at open mic events. She also lends her "voice" to community outreach, youth advocacy, and domestic violence awareness causes. Occasionally K`larity contributes as a guest blogger for various online magazines that cover topics related to women's health, youth and education and, of course, poetry.

As an Educator by trade, K`larity uses her artistic expression as a means of teaching and devotes much of her time to youth and family related services, such as counseling and mentoring. She has shared her talents with many non-profit organizations such as The YMCA of South Hampton Roads, VA and Teens With A Purpose (TWP) and its subsidiary Hampton Roads Youth Poets (HRYP).

K`larity is also an active participate within her church's youth and young adult ministries. With a genuine heart for people and a passion for life, she believes that everyone was designed for a specific purpose and it's up to that individual to allow their internal reflection to shine upon the world in a hugely unique way.

K`larity recalls an old saying, "I'm a voice in this world, and I deserve to be heard." It's the logic behind that statement that not only inspires her work with others, but it also fuels her energy and desire within. K`larity has always known that there was something very special and specific that she was born to fulfill. The ability to discern, comfort, and encourage are at the core of what makes K`larity's words "speak Life". She believes that her words shed a different light on life, offers clear insight, and challenges the listener to 'view' things another way.

    A very close friend believes K`larity's vision is defined within what she refers to as her life's verse that can be found in the Bible, 2 Corinthians 5:17. **"Therefore if anyone is in Christ he is a new creation; old things have passed away; behold, all things have become new.**

Contact Info:
www.twitter.com/poetikklarity
www.facebook.com/Klarity
www.myspace.com/klarity_517
Email- Sj2c517@gmail.com
On Youtube Klarity517

The Queen

Where can you find the Queen?
Well, the Queen can be seen in the beauty of Nature.
The Queen can be heard when the wind blows.
The Queen can be felt when love touches your heart.
The Queen can be observed performing the "Gift of Life".
The Queen can be mighty among few or stand out among the crowds.
The Queen can be down or simply down da block, around-the-way.
The Queen moves swiftly yet with careful steps, while changing her environment.
The Queen reigns within the community while campaigning our causes around the world—for it is her empire.
The Queen nurtures the mind of her King and cultivates the soil of her young.
Made of the ashes and dusts of the earth, yet more valuable than worth.
She's a hard rock, strong stone, can't be broken because she holds her own!
Like rubies, diamonds and pearls the Queen is a jewel.
Though many seek to refine her, others try to define her. Still our society denies her.
Instead, we settle for cheap imitations, man-made lab creations, of a gem.
When all the while she's been dwelling among them.
The Queen is not boastful, but she's proud.
She's proud of a legacy that tells of her greatness.
Descended from the heavens, manifested in the womb knows ALL because she's been here before.
Yet with each journey, she leaves behind something new, and something wonderful.
So, while the world slept she made some thousands of warriors that will continue on her name.
It's an uneven number, so it's odd to say that from one many remain,
But rest assured that SHE is real. For The Queen was just with you,
But if y'all blinked too fast you just missed her.
But when you question her existence, rest assured that SHE is real.

Black Pearl

"Wade in the Water."
Venture out into the sea so pure and deep.
"Wade in the Water."
Seek a buried treasure so majestic that's yours to keep
Go out and let the waves brush your skin.
Go on and let the waters rush you in.
If you travel a bit further you'll find 'em there.
They're waiting, existing, naturally without care.
Beauty formed from the earth's pain and sand.
Authentic beauty not made by hand.
Secretly sought after.
Frequently fought after.
Uncovered and perceived dirty.
Discovered and deemed worthy.
These gems of the Nile, all the while
Have a glow that's lustrous.
These sub terrain daughters of the Mediterranean waters
Are built marvelous and created flawless.
Gazing at a sight to behold
That others used, abused, auctioned and sold.
Protective exterior made to endure.
Objective interior made to secure.
Her valued virginity and priceless purity
Despite it all, she still shines,
Radiating her light given from the divine.
She remains firm when facing adversity,
Whole when fighting diversity.
She remains calm when combating the adversary
Knowing the struggle is necessary.
Surviving submersion, she raises up
Choosing conversion, her praises go up.
Removed from the shell and now set free.
Released from the bondage to live and just be.
No more looking back, no longer feeling trapped

By the weight of the world
No more tears to cry, no longer questions why.
She was born to take form and made a Black Pearl.

Un-Chained Butterfly

There's this song in my heart that sings of you.
There's this soul in part that belongs to you.
Behind the pain dwells the pleasure.
Within each tear lies the treasure.
It longs for Love and sees the sorrow.
It speaks of joy and embraces tomorrow.
Like a butterfly captured by innocence
Its image fades and changes in an instant.
It searched for you beneath & below.
Travel'n miles with scars left to show.
An oasis of hope, a mirage of relief,
Illusions of love that fade as I reach.
I can't look back and wonder why
Because I need to focus and clear my mind.
I won't think back and question how
Because I have to understand where I am now.
I held on to a love that we couldn't contain.
We built on a love that I couldn't sustain.
It was lovely to see, beautiful to mold.
It was exciting to me, a vision to behold.
But maybe that's why, maybe that's it.
Like trying to catch a butterfly that's free in spirit.
It needs to expand, it needs to soar.
It needs to be loved and so much more.
It needs sometime and needs some space.
It needs to discover the power of grace.
It needs to fall and crack its wings.
It needs to heal with a new song to sing.
It needs to wait and prepare for flight.

It needs to weep and endure for a night.
It needs to laugh and needs to smile.
It needs to trust and relax for a while.
So, that in the stillness and in the peace
The hurt has stopped, The hurt was released.

Even A Rose

She said she could build a shrine out of her tears.
That she's cried out **all** of these years.
Piled high with mounted fears, surpassing time and counting the years.
Just wanting him to love her, but soon she would discover
That hatred from another slowly takes over and places all else above her.
Her smile is behind an alias, often designed to disguise us
To get by from the pain of those who despised us.
So she goes into her subconscious to unlock what's inside us,
The remains of what hides us and reveals the truth.
Exposed the 'cute' that grows dead fruit.
The unclear appears, the mere scrimmage of a mirror image.
Yet I chose **YOU**, Developed like a rose to
Internally groom you. Develop and bloom through.
Growing from the hole in me, glowing from the soul to see.
Relentlessly, I endlessly await your light.
Shine upon me. Place mine above thee and illuminate the night.
Soul tie, Oh, my! How I need you.
I inhale the bare because nothings there when I breathe you.
Particles and dust, betrayals and lust are what remain.
Tragedy drying out. Dying out drastically and now here's the stain.
One drop, a single trace of a tear, a signal place stating you were here.
A crimson tattoo, mental prisons of taboo
Reaching up, Reaching out when what I really wanted was you.
So, relentlessly, I sprout my roots.
Rediscover myself, my worth and my truth.
Budding out from the shadow that was cast by you.

Expanding my stem. New smells, places, and touches.
I embrace **EVERYONE** of them in spite of you.
Nurtured and watered, cultivated and planted my own daughters.
Seed bearers, self-sufficient and self-confident. No need for care-ers.
So, again, relentlessly I branched out towards you.
Expanded out before you and it's, now, plain to see
That because of you I have risen stronger, taller with resiliency.

E.M.S. / Detox

A faded picture in a shattered frame.
Dreams and moments are all that remain.
Still remember your name, but the memory ain't the same.
When it lost focus, I never stopped to notice.
How soon things change and how 'cool' becomes strange.
An emotional strain to carry and maintain.
This mental baggage and spiritual pain.
Being me was easy with no hassle.
Free ME for release from these shackles.
Climbing the walls from going through withdrawals.
Fighting emotionally to purge my system.
Fighting mentally the urge to call or miss him.
Fighting spiritually to emerge from victim.
Having late night confessions about mid-day depressions.
Dispose my false security, expose my true identity.
Finding sentimental relief once blind from experimental beliefs
That emotionally supported this courtship.
Mentally distorted this relationship.
Spiritually aborted this friendship.
Though there were times I won't forget and words I don't regret.
It's no longer confusing me
Because now I'm choosing me!
Completely, emotionally, mentally, spiritually.

FREE

Like a bird I soar higher on your word.
I inhale your "air" and transport my soul every and anywhere.
I think of you the way you think of me.
I focus on you and my mind, body, and soul are set free.

Family Tree

There's this tree on my back that's making me weak.
There's this tree on my back which roots run deep.
There's this tree on my back with family secrets to keep.
There's this tree on my back that won't let my soul speak.
There's this tree on my back, and for salvation it seeks.
This tree I tried to carry used to be lost, but now it's found.
This tree I cried to bury lingers a sound.
Whispers so loud, with silence so proud
It cracked the sky and shattered the ground.
Engraved within the bark, an enslaved beauty mark.
Unsightly blemishes braved in the dark.
Many years counted from the bruises inside.
Many fears mounted from the confusion inside.
Infuriated thrashes, emancipated lashes,
Leaving behind liberated ashes.
Freed from self-inflictions, relieved from self-restrictions,
Released from self-convictions.
Removed from emptiness, restored from compromise.
Shattered chances, severed ties, broken branches and unspoken lies.
A tree often ignored and taken for granted,
But when I walked by the shore, there it was planted.
Removed from the tomb, removed from the garden.
Removed from the womb, where the soil hardened.
Removed to discover a new place of rest.
Removed to uncover a new space to bless.

New seeds to water, new seeds to sow
New minds to feed, new minds to grow.
Thirsty for knowledge, hungry for change
I invested in fruit where the truth remains.
Aspirations of encouragement, generations of empowerment.
Engulfed in life and the joy that surrounds.
Embraced in love and the peace I found
Surrendered my will and eased my tree down.
Surrendered my will, bowed my head and received my crown.

Washed Away

When life's scars left a stain
He washed them away and His blood remained.
A drift through life from day to day.
Riding the waves as He washes away
What holds me back and burdens my way.
He lifted the weight and washed it away.
The thoughts that I had from words I didn't say.
He renewed my mind and washed them away
When I got lost and went astray.
His footprints carried me the rest of the way.
When I gave up and turned away
He removed my dirt and washed it away.
For every time that I lied
And every hurt tucked inside,
For every tear that I cried,
Behind every smile that I hide.
From night to day
He cast them aside and washed them away.
For every time that I weep
From every secret I keep and the painful truth I speak.
It's Him that I seek.
It's His peace that's released and my soul is set free.
I'm able to smile and face the day

Because He came down and washed it away.
For every time I tried to deceive You.
For every time I didn't believe You.
For every time my doubts have grieved You.
For every regret and indecision.
For every worry I forgot to mention.
For everything I did to bring You disgrace.
For every wrong that can't be erased.
For every loss that can't be replaced.
For Your love and mercy within Your embrace.
For every moment of every day.
For forgiveness spared through Your Grace.
For every and any, the few and the many
He washed it away.

I Wanna

I wanna finish where I left off last night.
I wanna bring up new topics and give them some light.
I wanna clear the air and make sure we're still alright,
But then again I wanna know if we share the same insight.
I wanna relax my thoughts and give myself a break.
I wanna discuss and relate, de-code and separate.
I wanna feel the real and let go of the fake.
I wanna say things one way, hear them another.
I wanna say things today and tomorrow we still love each other.
I wanna share your pain and offer comfort to sustain.
I wanna look into your eyes and let out my cries.
I wanna feel free from drama, stress, and the lies.
I wanna lay it all down and back up from the table.
I wanna grow with a true friend who's willing and able.
I wanna know you from the inside out.
I wanna know your whole story and what you're really about.
I wanna build on visions that only you and I can see.
I wanna build on dreams until they're reality.
I wanna know what you think about that.
I wanna know where your head is at.
I wanna know how your heart reacts.
I wanna know if your soul fits mine exactly.
I guess I wanna know if you and I have compatibility.
Actually, I just wanna know the possibility.
I really wanna know answers to these questions I've had lately.

Lyrically Speaking

When I'm away from you, the moments pass too slowly.
Each second in time has surpassed eternity.
When we're apart I busy my mind with memories.
They pass in and out, calm and free like a soft breeze.
When we connect it's like lightning and thunder.
Explosive, electric, and full of wonder.
I reach peaks as high as mountains.
I flow freely into a bottomless fountain.
Yes, when we connect it's like we collide.
Releasing everything that's trapped inside.
You complete my sentences and form my words
You understand my thoughts that only silence heard.
You challenge my spirit and give it flight.
You inspire my soul to feel songs to write.
When we're not together nothing seems right,
But when we unite there's a spark that ignites.
A passion in my soul that smiles bright and radiates this true love.
The love of my life.

Evolutionary Soldier

I spit for the unsung warrior, the overlooked and ignored soldier.
The ones with all guts, but no glory.
The strong voices of an untold story.
The trailblazers of the beaten path,
the hell-raisers left in the aftermath
The one plus one equal three to none.
The undefined "classified" without an ad.
A history erased and all they had.
So, I emerged from the ash, with the Panther and The Lash.
It's evolutionary, so I redefined the dictionary.
I proceed, spring forth from the seed of a revolutionary.
'Cause essentially, they want us all gone eventually.
If I ruled the world and reigned from the throne
I'd raise my fist for solidarity to exist.
Take back and reclaim my own people
who've been denied, wept and died,
deceived and connived by evil.
YES! I am she, descended from he,
an external extension and connection of we.
The few and the many, the chosen and unsure.
The remnant of plenty, the stolen souls washed ashore.
The starved and the hungry, the tired and the thirsty.
Those whose names lay claim to unworthy.
The headless horsemen, midnight watchmen that move in the night,
by the light provided.
Go-get'rs and flow-spitters, verbal assassins
and un-veiled black masked men.
Plots and schemes.
This American dream is more to endure than what it seems.
So, I fight 'til it changes and I write to rearrange it.
Lyrically and mentally 'cause spiritually it was written and therefore meant to be.
I AM daily HIStory, not one month and lunar days
a calendar year that sooner fades.

I speak with the heart of those who dared and cared to be brave.
Stood their ground, stood tall and stood proud
and refused to be silent when the violent were loud.
I talk up for them who couldn't talk back.
I walk for them who were often sent back.
To the end of the line so I'll keep speaking for 'em and writing the rhyme.
Elevating souls and liberating minds until the end of time.

Anwar L. Counts

Anwar L. Counts is an author, actor and activist from Plainfield, New Jersey. Counts has three published collections of poetry. Birth of a Poet Conceived: The Womb of Difference (c) 2007, Youniqueness (c) 2008, Eyedentity (c) 2009. A fourth to be released early 2012 is Resurrected Poet: Reflection of HiStory.

Counts' writing expands to poetry, short-story, non-fiction, play and screen writing. Counts is also a writer, director, and producer of short-films, tv shows, PSA's and documentaries. Currently, Counts is the President of the United Youth Council, Incorporated (UYC) and member of Reverend Al Sharpton's National Action Network (NAN).

www.AnwarLCounts.webs.com
www.UnitedYouthCouncil.org

(An) Urban Legend

Have you ever heard of the urban legend
About the first man cured of AIDS?
It happened early 1990s
Back in African apartheid days
They say, he went for a checkup that day
Didn't know that it would turn into a hospital stay
The doc ran some test and came to a conclusion
The man was a diabetic in need of a blood transfusion
There was confusion; he didn't know what to say
He did what he did in those situations:
Look to God and prayed
No teasers would drain
He showed strength instead
He had a dream that night in the hospital bed
All was well on operation day
That was before the doc came to say,
We have some good news and some bad,
Which do you prefer first?
The man said, Give me the good, save me the worst
The operation went as planned all, but one thing
What's that?
Take a breath because this may sting
Your blood was good, our blood was bad
What are you saying, doc?
Please, sir, I know you'll be mad
Bet you I can take it well you'll be amazed
Well, sir, sadly, you have AIDS
What? How? What do you mean?
Your blood was good, our blood was bad
I think you can fill-in the between
There was confusion; he didn't know what to say
He did what he did in those situations
Look to God and prayed
No tears would drain.

Black Like Me

I want a Jesus, Black, like me
That's the type of picture I'd like to see
That's the type of story I'd like to hear
That's the type of man I'd likely fear
A Jesus, Black, like me
I want a Jesus, Black, like me
And though my skin isn't the blackest
I'd like to see Jesus baptized by a brown
John the Baptist
Hold hands with the yellow man
Pray for the red man
Look out for the white man
In the mirror
See a Black man
I want to be the reflection of He
Created in His image
I want a Jesus Black like me
Punished, punctured, whipped in His back
I, punished, punctured, whipped for being black
He showed us a way, the way to behold
I followed the way of the Underground Railroad
His blood was drained to set us free
My blood was drained in slavery
He hung from a cross
I, from a tree
He forgave a thief
He can accept me
I want a Jesus, Black, like me
That's the type of picture I'd like to see
That's the type of story I'd like to hear
That's the type of man I'd likely fear
A Jesus, Black, like me.

Eyedentity

Look in the mirror. Who do you see?
The person you are, or who you want to be?
An image of greatness, or one of misery?
If I face the mirror is the image me?
Look in the mirror. What do you see?
That which is there, or all given possibilities?
An image of your pride, or one of humility?
Is this image your guide,
An angel by your side,
Or, one internally?
If I face the mirror does the image reflect me?
Look in the mirror. Who do you see?
Are they a face of beauty?
Is it who you are truly?
Are they perfect in every way?
Is it who you are just today?
If I face the mirror, then who faces me?
Look in the mirror. What do you see?
The image is your originality
An irreplaceable image
Allowing you to be
The image
Is your destiny
If I face the mirror then I see me
I see... My Eyedentity.

Hopping the Fence

Off to the races
Hopping the fence
Chasing your dollars
While working for cents
Slugging his plunger
Twisting his wrench
Climbing the ladder
Hopping the fence
Hammers his hammer
Bites his nails
Not the ones on his fingers
Bangs his fingers and yells
His language is foreign
His culture is different
Landlords don't know what to call him
His license, green card, insurance is non-existent
They look for suggestions
Try to make sense
Turn their backs, turn back, and see him
Hopping the fence
His clothes are torn
His thermos is filled
His pockets are light
Just determined with will
Strokes his brush
Has an artist's touch
A Jackal and Carpenter
As he sweeps up dust
Know not what they say
See what they do
Little to nothing
Little to nothing for you a love from one to all
Rain, sleet, or snow when he's drenched
Day rise, nightfall – see him

Hopping the fence
He may be imprisoned,
Deported, battered, or bruised
He is more than all for it
He would be embarrassed to lose
Not embarrassed at all
To do what you refuse
He works with pride
Swallows it and, when needed, he chews
Borders are watched
Broken as levees and junkies
Overflowing of outsourced
Workers inbound the country
He hops as he chooses
All 'cause he can
Cross over the border
Onto Freedom Land
Off to the races
Hopping the fence
Chasing your dollars
While working for cents
Slugging his plunger
Twisting his wrench
Climbing the ladder
Hopping the fence.

I am who I am

I am who I am
I am not he or she
I am not you
I am who I am to be
Accept me as I am
Good God has a plan
Written is my lifespan
With the "power of choice"
I choose to be me
I am who I am
Who you may think I am
May not be
Not a saint
A thinking man
Not religious traditionally
Influenced spiritually
Fear: God, death, mystery
My yesterday's future
Is my today's present
To be,
My tomorrow's history
My journey and destiny
A character in Life
My life in spite
My troubles and dislikes
My mistrust and wrong-rights
My personality, looks and height
My weight, gain and hindsight
My success, failure and advice
My fate, myself, my life
I am who I am
I am not he or she
I am not you
I am who I am to be

I am me
Fruition of my *Eyedentity*

Miracle of a Dream

What do you want to do?
Who do you want to be?
The boy you are, or the man you see?
The girl you are, or woman you're trying to be?
The choice between the two may present option number three
All eyes on you. Now, what will it be?
Close your eyes
Fall fast asleep
Lost in the moment
Can't find your feet
Step to the sound
Music of your heartbeat
Accept ya' crown
Fit ya' like a car seat
Drive to success
Inspired you seem
Open your eyes
You've acquired a dream
Motivate the masses
A challenge it is
Celebrate the classics
All the sounds of the dead
Liberate enslaved minds
Remind my kind of slave times
Front of the line; no more signs,
Telling me to move back or behind
Fist raised representing unity
You, me, us, we, dually

Together we shall see
As it would seem
The miracle of a dream

My Brother's Keeper

I am my brother's keeper!
I am my brother's keeper!
My brother's keeper
My brother's keeper
My brother's keeper
I'm trying to build, my brother
Not trying to kill, my brother
Let's keep it real, my brother
Tell you how I feel, my brother
I'm from the field, my brother
"Queen City" where they steal from mothers
Stolen life doesn't heal with covers
Fathers, beware, my brother
Because, some of us don't care, my brother
Misguided, call them "gangs", but they stays my brother
On the block, on the corner, where they hangs my brother
I know it's life that they slain, my brother
But, we can't let it maintain, my brother
I'm going insane, my brother!
Slave mentality done came, my brother
We can't let it remain, my brother
It's time for this to change, my brother
My brother, I love ya'
Love ya' brothers
My brother's keeper
I am my brother's keeper!
I am my brother's keeper!
My brother's keeper.

Opportunity

Marylyn Monroe is Halle Berry today
Sounds of sweet music coming from the lips,
Of Billie Holiday
I can see Josephine Baker dance
When I give Debbie Allen a glance
I can see Cicely Tyson act
When Angela Basset has an on-screen
Emotional asthma attack
Waiting to Exhale
Waiting for Whitney Houston to get well
And blow again,
Without all the "blow" she was in
Madame C.J. Walker gave a perm to curls
Today, Queen Latifah is a Cover Girl
Oprah Winfrey is a role model
Tyra Banks is an ex-fashion show model
Both are showing girls a role to follow
From Hattie McDaniel to Halle Berry's win
There I go with Halle Berry again
Thinking of modern Black Hollywood
Saying the names anybody else would:
Denzel, Terrance,
Don, Forrest, Will, Lawrence,
Fishburn—astounding as Morpheus
Morgan is another that brings force to flicks
Spike shooting to roll a big joint
Cuba expressing emotion to show his point
Ottis Redding, Mahalia Jackson, Nat King Cole,
Quincy Jones—Motown
Back when music had its soul
Earth, Wind, and Fire,
Isley Brothers,
Temptations, "Four Tops?"
One of the groups mentioned

At a Steve Harvey comedy spot
Jennifer Holiday to Jennifer Hudson
Supremes plus Dream Girls equal Major Production
Actors, Singers and Comedians
From Pam Grier, Beyonce to Monique
Sound and sight, reaching all the mediums
To all the voices who can't speak
To all the ears who can't hear
And all the eyes who can't see
All the inspiration in the world
Opportunity to be
Anybody
You can be
Anybody
You want to be
Be yourself, be *you*nique.

Reflection of HiStory

The place from whence you came, you didn't have to flip cocaine.
Spit mad game. You were rich with no fame.
You knew the exact pronunciation of your name .
When they asked
As of now you don't know your name
Since hatred has stolen your past
Still, you hold fast
May hold no cash yet when they pull your card
They'll see all the goals you have
Worth more than the gold mines
You are a possessor of a gold mind
Keep your face in the sky
You'll always shine
Just remember to be conscious
of the reflection of what went on behind
Review the rearview--that pictures history.

Youth is Gold(en)

Youth is new
Youth ain't old
Youth is fresh
Youth is gold
Youth is bliss
Youth is ignorance
Youth is life
When it's first commenced
Youth abides
Youth consents
Youth may lie
But, youth is innocence
Youth is chaste
Youth is well
Youth don't waste
Youth is just a spell
Youth is the future
Youth is the present
Youth is a gift
Youth is the essence
Youth is precious
Youth is free
Youth is genuine
Youth is to be
Youth is new
Youth ain't old
Youth is fresh
Youth is gold
Youth is golden.

K. L. Belvin

K. L. Belvin is a prime example of what happens when you allow God to take control of your life. A father of six, High School Dean of students for the New York City Department of Education for over twelve years.

K. L. is the Co-founder, along with his wife, Tiffany Braxton Belvin of Bravin Publishing. Under their company KL released his first manuscript titled "A Man in Transition," a book of poems, stories and personal observations. With the success of the first book, Keith released his memoir "From Gigolo to Jesus" in 2011. It discusses his journey from being a manwhore to a man of God.

K. L. is also a co-host of Black Love Radio; an internet radio show dedicated to bringing focus to rebuilding relationships and "Making Marriage Cool Again".

In addition to being an author and publisher KL is also a motivational speaker and life coach.

THE DEATH OF THE RADICALS

Where have the individuals gone who saw the world differently? How the hell did we lose the fight when so many use to line up in a belief of a common right? True radicals would never be swayed by the lure of World Star Hip Hop or MEDIA TAKE OUT. Our children's lives use to mean more than three minutes of fame. We should be ashamed of the books we read. There was a time fingers in the dirt was how we passed the knowledge of written words. Back when we cherished reading more than life. Now the top booksellers benefit on speaking about lifestyles most don't want or many don't care to live over, yet we keep buying. Damn!

Who murdered the internal connection to the Huey Newtons, Bobby Seals, Malcolm Xs, Rosa Parks, Dr. Martin Luther King Jr., and so many well know, but easily forgotten sprits. It was Harriet Tubman who uttered, "I can't die, but once." Doesn't your soul scream in disgust or do you drown it out with music which doesn't represent anything positive? Yet we keep piling into concert after concert giving "those who don't look like us" reason to laugh at how we enslave ourselves with strong sexual lyrics laced with violent overtones at the very Queens we need to produce more Kings.

When did Radicals die or did they run away? The true radical understood we were at war. If we couldn't live like men or women then death would be better. Now our children dress like pimps and whores gyrating on each other like animals in heat. The role of the radical was to grant ownership back to lost Kings and Queens yet we fight to continue to be serfs. A true radical studied and understood the power of a college education. Here we stand as they march us off to war or jail smiling as we pass around the flyers for the next big BBQ, Ski Trip, or Crab Fest, with "BYOBB" or "TOP SHELF" in extra large letters set in place to entice our attendance.

When was the funereal, was there a service for the late great super hero called the Radical? There was a time we stood for something. Even intertwined Malcolm X's phrase "If You Don't Stand For Something You'll Fall For Anything" into our daily understanding. Now we sit around using the internet to show off planking pictures because we want to one-up the ignorant negro planking on his roof just because.

My heart cries because when I mention this to most, I am called a sell-out, or too serious. We have allowed the term, "No Snitching" to hold more respect than "Black Power", "Unity", or "Freedom" in our neighborhoods. When did rappers, entertainers, and ball players start holding the ear of the people? Damn where are the radicals?

Our sons can now marry their brothers and our daughters their sister then ask their male friend for sperm to start families. It's all business as usual. Why did Black churches get so quiet the day the law was passed. It came and passed and it was ho-hum back to the business of saving souls. Did I miss something? The greatest radical ever seen was Jesus Christ yet the greatest disconnection comes from those who claim the love and follow him? Remember, when folks fought in attempts to prove He had "Skin of bronze and hair like wool? Are you kidding me? Hold that contradiction for a moment.

As I close, I wonder how the evil ones in the world got to the mountain top before the rest of us. Did they look over and see King's dream only to slither down and whisper into the ears of the masses climbing, "Kill the Radicals and all your dreams shall be fulfilled"? As a people, we have laid down for the count out, instead of continuing to fight and taking our chances.

I lay these flowers on the grave of the one known as the Radical. May You rest in peace you are surly missed.

Poetry Forgive Us

Excuse me my Queen, may I return to my seat at your table.
I look forward to this meal you have presented.
When I am done I'll tell others of the many tastes you've conjured.
Many have mistakenly lost the essence of your beauty.
I've seen so many attempts to court you while not paying the respect deserved one of nobility.
Your legacy is one of elegance, grace, pain, pleasure, love and hate.
Time has watched as you've danced enjoying your stay in this existence.
The children you've sired have taken up roots around the world.
Why have so many forgotten their home?
Some have sought to master you while changing your name as to not give credit to you.
We have seen you dressed in everything imaginable from gowns, to robes, to rags, to crowns.
Yet, your heart has been bruised, stabbed at with the way you've been forgotten.
The Creator gave us you as a gift and we act as if we held the role.
I ask you to forgive us who somehow sought to control your actions.
I pray the time will never come when you are absent from our midst.
As with all gifts, they are to be treasured.
I will display my own and do so until I no longer draw breath.
My lady, I will guard you and protect you by hiding you in my soul and in my heart.
Showing all what you mean to me.
I will beg all others who claim to respect you to fight for you; for if we lose you a part of all of us dies.
Wipe your tears. You are cared for; not all has forsaken you.
Poetry, we love you and ask your apology for how we've treated you.
Thank you for allowing me to sit at your table.

Racism

Don't we cry the same tears, but for different reasons? Haven't we both seen the smiles of our children when they were born? Doesn't our sun rise and set in the same way?

We both kneel and pray to the same God, or do we? We both want the same salvation when he returns. We both love our families with the force of a hurricane.

Both our hearts hurt when we are unable to provide for our loved ones. Our bodies run on the same fuel just seasoned differently. Hell, on certain days, given certain situations, we even listen to the same music.

Why does spilling my blood move you to excitement? Why does holding me back make you more of King then me? Where did the fear of who I could be cause you to try to destroy what I am or was?

Does my heritage hold the secrets that would summon the Lord back sooner? Is it guilt or frustration of what my body can do in space and time that sends fear through you? Does dulling my keen senses keep you safer?

How much drugs, wine, or poor education is enough for you to rest comfortable at night? How did the evil one convince you control of life and death is yours for the deciding?

You can't explain my speed, my might or conviction. You decided if the flame of who I am is ever truly released you would cease to exist.

Well, the time will come when you will answer for your crimes against me. We will both stand on judgment day and hear the words read back. Our tears will stream at the same time and our hearts will be filled with emotions. For at the same moment we will truly be equal.

Except, I'll kneel at the feet of the Great One saying, "I knew you wouldn't allow this pain to last forever." You'll kneel next to me saying, "I knew this day would come and I would pay for the pain I caused."

A DIVA
Dedicated to one of God's greatest gifts

With each sunrise, your smile greats the Creator.
His daughter is ready to meet the day.
Unlike any other, you're unique from head to toe.

Misunderstood by many, for your stature is envied and hated by others.
You carry the mantle of Queen.
You're a wondrous site to behold.

You don't walk you sway.
Each stride is an elegant glide
With your shoulders back and head held high.
We soak and bask in your sensual pride.

Your mind is a feature overlooked, but never played with.
You are the cradle of life.
For within you, the secrets of the past and songs of the future rest
waiting on release.

The world wouldn't be the same without your extra large frame.
What would we do if deprived of the daily vision of your full-bodied excellence?
Sister, you are Loved for you truly are;
A DIVA

I Would Say I Do All Over Again

Your smile brightens my world; sending messages God is real.
You're my Sarah, my Ruth, my Ester and my Mary.
With each look, I fall in love with you all over again.
Is this real? Of course it is.
As real as the day I joked, "Someday you'll be mine."
I told you we would be here.
Can you remember when I said
I'd be the greatest man you've ever known?
Who knew in my arrogance, I was speaking a word to what you'd bring to my life.
We've seen darkness, pain, and moments of despair.
There were times when ending this relationship would have been the common choice.
Our tears and moments of pain have always given way to a brighter tomorrow.
We have seen the light that followed the storms.
Together we prayed when there was nothing left for us to do.
Only to see those prayers answered.
I cherish each breath I am blessed to be with you.
Can you hear Toni Braxton and Johnny Gill singing us into holy matrimony as we stood with family and friends?
The sun, from our day, is still felt as the song signaled your arrival.
The pastor asked, "Do you Keith and do you Tiffany?"
Can you still feel the tears of joy as we uttered, "I DO!"
Remember how we faced down "Dean" with only our love and prayer?
Then refused to allow even a hurricane to pull us apart?
A year later, returned triumphant to the same spot with the echoes of that great wind whistling in the Jamaican breeze.
Husband and wife: the words are so common, but to us so special.
They can never mean to others what they mean to you and me.
I've sworn an oath to love you, cherish you, protect you, and even die for you if I have too.
Many don't understand and some will never comprehend what we have.
You see my Love; I wouldn't change a thing about you.

Today is our day; the day we became one.
The day the Lord set aside just for us.
Materials I don't have, wealth has yet to be given,
yet I am richer than a man can be because I have you.
Allow me to wish us peace and mercy
 in the presence of the world in the eyes of the Father.
No mere gift from me can express what we have.
You are my wife; the one the Lord has given me.
This is my gift; I stand and shout for all who will listen
and those who try not to.
From the bottom of my heart, I would say I do all over again.

-Husband of Tiffany Braxton Belvin

Transformation

The caterpillar moves into position.
The time reaches near; his end is the beginning.
How does he feel on the brink of oblivion?

We share the same existence as that caterpillar.
The vices, baggage, issues we carry come from the weight of contemplation.
If we are to conceive the newness, which is to be our future, we cannot resist the impending death of right now.

The womb is spun as the caterpillar assumes the position.
The cycle begins and magic is abounded.
Movement stills and the Creator whispers, "Sleep".

We step forward to address our internal bondage.
The cocoon is slowly closing, we ask openly, "Am I really ready for this?"
Deep inside the Great One sends word, "Leave that weight with me".

The butterfly springs forth with only the memories of its previous life.
He must face the world as the new creature he has become.
With each stroke of its wings, the change is complete.

It is time for the world to see the new you.
No wings as the butterfly, but a soul cleansed of the blockage.
With held high, chest pressed to the sun, arms raised, you are transformed.

Promises

It was this time of year when you said, "Don't worry baby I'll be there."
I stood staring out the stained window, waiting.
How could you not come and keep your word?
Like the other times you continue to kill my dreams.

Mom tries to comfort the pain, but it runs deep.
She was a victim of the same poison you're feeding me.
Here I am waiting on a Santa who apparently doesn't like children.
As each car passes, I feel a little less human.

What did I do? I didn't ask to be here.
You spoke those words so strong, so clear. I fell for it again.
Each year, I grow only to feel the same pain differently.
Why do you continue to steal my joy from me? My love for you is real.

The words "I have a gift for you" or
"You know I love you" has the taste of a curse.
Yet, I continue to hope and pray the Lord has pity on me.
On days like today I should be out in creation
enjoying this holiday season.
But all I do is fight off hate and your lies disguised as promises.

Let it Go!
(Ode to an Ex)

To hold a negative feeling hostage is the worst type of sickness. It's been too long, doesn't time heal all wounds? But what happens when the person doesn't know their sick? You pass this disease on to all who come in contact with you. Yet you blame others.
You're dying, slowly, and here you believe you're happy.
Your children can sense it. They dare not speak on it. Their silence is secured by the uneasiness of your behavior.
How long will you hold this gun to the head of anyone you deem unworthy? With each insult, quip your souls hardens. You are hollow.
You are quick to point out the flaws of others. However, subliminally, you remain perfect in every way. Love has a very different meaning to you. Those close to you hold to the hope change will come.
But you can't hear the music or the words of that song. You feel the world will pay for what it's done to you.
I pray for you because I was part of this transformation. I remember when you were without this pain.
Today, I don't understand why you cling to it like rope to a drowning man.
One day you'll awaken from your spiritual hibernation and see these days long past.
Old age and lost youth will be your prize for time wasted.
You will know what many a bitter person has learned.
Which is every step of this walk, called life, we will face these moments. You are not alone in what has happened in your trek of living. However, the price paid will be great when all you had to do from the start was let it go.

A Steward

Standing and facing the creator the question is simply, "Why did you pick me to be a steward of these lives you've given?"
You knew at that time I was so far from being a responsible man, yet you allowed life to flow through me.
From their mothers, I was after the romance and sexual feeling.
I was in it for the personal conquest trying to take possession of their being, possibly their soul.
Why did you sit back and watch me act opposite that which you are?
When you created me, you knew what I would become.
Why did you allow me to have heirs?
Why a bloodline with such a negative foundation?
These young beloved souls breathe life given by you and yet you curse them with a parent whose personal needs outweighed the concern for others.
What is your plan? Why would you do this?
Are you who you say you are?
You are perfect, and I am flawed beyond belief, yet you allowed me to become a father, why?
Day to night, night to day fighting this internal pain I carry and a small voice says stay faithful.
As I see my young ones grow and I learn more about You I see change. These bundles of joy, cradles of mystery cause the internal voice to grow louder, asking me these questions, similar to my own.

Did I not open a sea and allow men, women, and children to pass?
Did I not allow your brother—my son—to commit to death to submit to my will?
Haven't you seen the wonders of this world?
Remember who spoke light into a darkened void.
Have you not learned all will not be revealed at once, but only when its time.
Why do you have anger, concern, or fear at what should be a time of rejoicing?

You were chosen as an ambassador of the most high.

Through these little ones you will be able to right the wrongs done to you and which you've taken part in.
You see my son your bloodline is not evil. You come from me.
Your thoughts and intentions have been evil; however, I use everything I create for good.
In this position I have given you, move to focus on more than yourself.
Do you now begin to see the perfection?
I am rewarding you; I am offering you another way out from the cloak of destruction you were resting under.

The Voice grows quiet as my tears stream along my face.
I begin to understand.
My children are my chance to introduce my heavenly Father to this world, hence reconnecting to Him, myself.
If I am successful, I'll save more than just my life, but possibly a family and its future. The answers to my questions are not needed they have been given in the blessings of my children and my role as their father.
I kneel and say thank You for choosing me to be a steward of these young ones.

To my son, Jonathan Stewart, who after 26 years found me.

We have the same blood, same face and pray to the same God, who knew that each night we were asking for the same things, but in different places. Close enough to speak yet far enough to pass by quietly you grew older as I did the same. Same hood, same mentors, same people, but at different times and different eras the path you traveled was sprinkled with reminders of who I was and who I am. We shared the same whisper, same code of honor and the same inner voice connected us to the Father. Who knew the time when our journey would come full circle? Same pride, same smile and same heart who knew that someday, the Son would find his Father and in turn find God. Who knew? I'll tell you my son, God knew all the time. It's never about why. It's about when and what you do when the "When" happens.

God Bless you.

www.ingramcontent.com/pod-product-compliance
Lightning Source LLC
LaVergne TN
LVHW041622070426
835507LV00008B/405